Across Cultures and Empires

Across Cultures and Empires

An Immigrant's Odyssey from the Soviet Army to the US War in Iraq and American Citizenship

Mahir Ibrahimov

University Press of Kansas

All photographs are from the author's personal collection.

Views presented herein are those of the author and do not necessarily represent those of the US Department of Defense or its components.

Published by the University Press of Kansas (Lawrence, Kansas 66045), which was organized by the Kansas Board of Regents and is operated and funded by Emporia State University, Fort Hays State University, Kansas State University, Pittsburg State University, the University of Kansas, and Wichita State University.

Library of Congress Cataloging-in-Publication Data

Names: Ibrahimov, Mahir, 1956– author.
Title: Across cultures and empires : an immigrant's odyssey from the Soviet Army to the US war in Iraq and American citizenship / Mahir Ibrahimov.
Description: Lawrence, Kansas : University Press of Kansas, 2021. | Includes bibliographical references.
Identifiers: LCCN 2020044315
ISBN 9780700632237 (cloth)
ISBN 9780700632244 (epub)
Subjects: LCSH: Ibrahimov, Mahir, 1956– | Azerbaijani Americans—Biography. | Diplomats—Azerbaijan—Biography. | Nagorno-Karabakh Conflict, 1988–1994. | Soviet Union. Sovetskaia Armiia—Biography. | Iraq War, 2003–2011—Personal narratives, American. | United States. Army—Civilian employees—Biography. | Translators—Iraq—Biography.
Classification: LCC E184.A94 I26 2020 | DDC 956.7044/3092 [B]—dc23
LC record available at https://lccn.loc.gov/2020044315.

British Library Cataloguing-in-Publication Data is available.

Printed in the United States of America

10 9 8 7 6 5 4 3 2 1

The paper used in this publication is recycled and contains 30 percent postconsumer waste. It is acid free and meets the minimum requirements of the American National Standard for Permanence of Paper for Printed Library Materials Z39.48-1992.

Contents

Prologue
Deadly Day

The US Air Base, Balad, Iraq, June 2004

I came back to the unit earlier than usual that day. The security situation was up and down all the time. We had mortar and rocket attacks several times a day. Tragedy was happening randomly and, unfortunately, we were getting used to it. But the tragedy of June 16, 2004, shocked all of us. We knew that we would remember it for the rest of our lives.

I had just come back from work when I realized that I needed to buy some toothpaste. I was about to leave my place to go to the store when I suddenly felt very tired and decided to lie down for a while. When I woke up an hour and a half later, I finally left to go to the store. As I approached the building, I noticed a crowd of people gathered around. It was the looks of shock and fright on their faces that made me realize what had happened.

A war is made up of thousands of stories of loss and pain. For instance, I know that after the first round of a rocket attack hit the base on June 16, 2004, a group of soldiers and contractors left the safety of the military store before the typical "all clear" siren sounded. Four soldiers were killed and about twenty-five were wounded when a second rocket fell.

Sergeant M. was one of the four soldiers killed during that attack. He had just left the internet café, where he had been looking for tickets and hotel space for him and his family. His extended fifteen-month assignment in Iraq was coming to an end. In fact, M. was supposed to arrive home the following day and be reunited with his family. June 16, 2004, was supposed to be the last day that Sergeant M. spent away from his family. Instead, it was his final day.

A female soldier from his unit was at the nearby call center when she heard the blast. She rushed to the scene and saw Sergeant M. lying on the ground with a piece of shrapnel lodged in his throat. As he lay there dying, the female soldier pretended to be a medical nurse from the hospital and held M.'s hand, comforting him in his last minutes.

In war, it is possible for there to be stories of miracles mixed in with the stories of loss and pain. As tragic as this incident was, it was a miraculous moment for me. If I had not fallen asleep after work, I would have been buying toothpaste at the exact spot where that rocket fell. I could have been one of the wounded or dead. Suddenly feeling tired and falling asleep probably saved my life. I owe more to fate than I can ever repay. When this kind of incident happens, you start rethinking your entire life. How and why did I end up in Iraq in the first place? Would another twist of fate lead me to the type of tragedy that I had just barely missed? Or did I think that this kind of incident would never happen to me? The nasty and brutal realities of the war became a part of my yearlong Iraqi experience. It was an experience that would change my life forever.

The Iraq War would be part of my life and experiences many years later, though there were many other wars, tragedies, and experiences that had preceded it.

1

Soldier of the Empire

Beginning of the End

December 1974, Soviet Military School, Volzhskiy, Outskirts of the Volgograd Oblast, Russia, Union of Soviet Socialist Republics (USSR)

My hands were outstretched before me, an uncontrolled reflex to protect my face. The soft inner center took the brunt of the blow bestowed by the frozen ground, but my arms buckled under the force and a sharp pain shot through my cheek, under my left eye. Something, probably a rock, had cut me. I felt it rip into my skin, and then I felt the warm blood as it rolled down my face. I did not move for a moment, unsure of how I had tripped. My mind began a quick body check, registering first my head and down through my limbs, scanning the parts for injury. All clear—just my hands and face. A shadow appeared on the ground in front of me; I turned my head to see a steel-tipped boot forcing itself between two of my ribs. The pain didn't register until the foot withdrew. I looked up and saw a thin, dark circle of brown encasing a kaleidoscope of blue-green colors in an iris that, had there been some sense of humanity behind it, would have been stunning. The face, too, was pretty, surrounded by spikes of short dark hair. In the space of seconds, before the second blow hit, I wondered if the others teased him, if it was difficult to be a pretty boy in command of an army unit.

"Up!"

I didn't move.

"Up!"

Maybe it was the cold or perhaps the pain; I still saw those eyes, but the face seemed transformed, tortured, even ugly.

A third blow, this time to my kidney. As I collapsed, my chest slammed hard into the ground. I gasped, searching for the air that had escaped from my lungs. My fingers clawed the rocks and pebbles surrounding me, expressing the agony I could not vocalize. My backpack fell to my side and kept me off-balance. I had to shift the weight before I could roll onto my hands and knees and stand. In order to do that, I had to twist the parts of my torso that had just been battered. Each turn was greeted by paralyzing pain. The blood continued to run down the side of my face, and my eye was beginning to swell. As I looked down, I could see dark wet drops on the snow-dusted surface. I pulled up my knees and got onto all fours, trying to reposition my backpack. I overcorrected, it shifted again, and I teetered over, about to fall.

Then came another blow. A second officer decided to join the fun and struck me with the heel of his boot. It had the unintended effect of centering my backpack, and I scrambled to my feet. I took a wild swing in the air. It felt as if my cracked rib was tearing into my muscle. The pretty boy laughed, grabbed my arm, twisted it, and pushed me into the second officer, who shoved me back down. My arms failed me again and my face smacked back onto the ground. I heard a crack and yelped as rings of pain rippled between my eyes.

Some time passed. It might have been only seconds, maybe minutes; I don't know. My mind wandered to a place outside. Finally, I turned my head and saw indistinct brown shapes and shadows that slowly bent and swayed in and out of focus. Sounds were garbled, and the volume turned down low. My nostrils filled with fluid, so I gulped, trying to force air into my lungs. Instead, my mouth filled with blood, and I gagged. My tongue ballooned in size so that when I tried to spit, pushing my tongue forward from the back of my throat, I made sort of a puckering sound, like when a rubber stopper is pulled from a drain. An officer still standing near me kicked me in the thigh for good measure and walked off. I stayed there for a while. No other soldiers came to my aid. They watched without looking directly at me and moved away, creating a safety zone between them and me. I don't blame them. The average age in my unit was nineteen. Everyone was scared, and no one wanted to become the next victim. I had to get up. The ground had about as much give as a slab of marble so that laying chest down did not allow for much breathing space. I did and continued the exercise.

The whole "evil empire" tale concocted here in the United States at the time was a bit overdone, but it was a dead-on description of the Soviet army. Life in the Soviet army was filled with arbitrary acts of brutality. More soldiers died during the basic training of the troops in the Soviet Union than in any of the Western countries. Cause of death: barbarism, or, more accurately, *dedovshchina* (from the Russian "ded" [grandfather], and literally meaning "grandfathership"), which was the violent use of power by officers and senior conscripts against new recruits. Today it is considered a crime, but in 1974, it was an open secret masked by taboo, not to mention formal military cover-ups. All attempts at forcing military accountability for the dedovshchina were countered with accusations of drunkenness and cowardice on the part of the victim. Soldiers were viewed as expendable manpower; at one point, there were estimates that one soldier per day died as a result of dedovshchina, putting soldiers at greater risk of death during peacetime training than during wartime combat. Headstones of the poor souls who died were inscribed: "Died heroically in the performance of his internationalist duty."[1] There were no avenues of redress; Soviet soldiers had fewer rights than Soviet prisoners. The truth is, despite all efforts at homogenization, the Soviet Union was a deeply ethnic place. To my compatriots and to my comrades, I was defined by my heritage, but according to the government, I was a citizen of the Union of Soviet Socialist Republics, and it was my sacred duty to provide "my country" with two years of army service.

I was Azerbaijani, which made me a non-Russian, or, more accurately, a Caucasian—one who lived in the Caucasus, which included Georgia, Armenia, Azerbaijan, and various parts of Russia. There was an unofficial hierarchy between the Russians and non-Russians. The Russians were treated with greater respect. Non-Russians were subjected to the vitriol of the officers; we were the dregs, the untouchables. The Russians hailing from Siberia and the Far East were the most athletic and oftentimes the cruelest. They created *zemliachestvo* or *gruppovshchina*—ethnic bonding—their own enclave within the unit that persecuted other ethnic groups, causing more pain and injury in a situation that was already fraught with both.

Although education may not be the measure of a man, it did seem to shine a light on civility. The more senior the soldier and the less educated he was, the more monstrous the behavior. I am not sure intelligence is a valued commodity in any rank-and-file soldier, but critical thinking and independence were not only discouraged in the Soviet Union, they were dangerous.

Azerbaijan was a reluctant member of the Soviet Union. The Red Army invasion of 1920 persuaded that small country to relinquish its dreams of democracy that had birthed only two years earlier. And I was a reluctant soldier, having been conscripted into service only two months after I had won a hard-fought battle to enter Baku Medical College's technical dentistry program. Worse was the injustice of it, since mandatory army service was normally waived for all those attending school at the university level.

By law, every able-bodied Soviet man between the ages of eighteen and twenty-seven was eligible for military duty and expected to serve at least two years. Only a fraction of them actually did. Favored methods of avoiding the draft included false medical certificates and bribes. Only the poor and the poorly connected actually had to serve.

Twice a year, once in the spring and once in the autumn, there was a call-up of new conscripts. I received my draft notice by letter in November 1974.

During the call-ups, the government engaged in a mass-propaganda campaign. It was all pomp, circumstance, and breasts. Young men were leaving the bosoms of their mothers to be embraced by the bosom of the supreme mother of them all: the Soviet Union. All that talk of patriotism appealed to my blossoming manhood. I sucked it up like a dry sponge so that when I was offered a less strenuous job in a construction unit, because of my flat feet, I refused, insisting that I wanted a real army experience.

They sent me to one of the most difficult units, located in one of the harshest places in Russia: Volgograd, formerly Stalingrad. Stalingrad holds the infamous distinction of hosting the costliest military battle in human history. It is credited with serving as a pivotal point in the Second World War for the allies. The cost of that victory: almost four million people killed or wounded. Despite enormous death and destruction, the people of Volgograd wear the distinction as a badge of honor. The defining characteristic is the statue *Mamayev Kurgan* (Мамаев курган, the Motherland Calls) overlooking the city. It memorializes the World War II battle and the inhabitants of the hero city, so designated by the presidium of the USSR Supreme Soviet. At the time of its completion in 1967, Mamayev Kurgan was the largest statute in the world—a two-hundred-and-eighty-foot-tall, eight-thousand-ton concrete and steel metaphor for war.[2] She is a woman filled with terror and violence, draped in classical Greek garb, wielding a ninety-foot sword. Her mouth is open, screaming the cry to battle. Her arched eyebrows are etched in hatred, and her Medusa-like shoulder-length hair is swept up and sideways in a wild and winded frenzy. Her enormous, thick-girthed arms are open, embracing death. Like the politicians who control the wars, her back is turned so that she does not face the city and the people who live there. The Mamayev Kurgan is a vertical victory parade, all glory and no gore; her stone eyes are open, but just like all of the celebrants at the parade, she has never really seen a war.

Ugly though she is, the Mamayev Kurgan is the single most memorable artifact of Volgograd. A modern-day internet travel guide describes Volgograd as "not very nice" but "with a few interesting spots."[3] It goes on to recommend a walk along the promenade on the banks of the Volga River and a view of the local power plant. Volgograd is, however, presently featured in internet sites for those seeking Russian brides.[4]

I was actually stationed in Volzhskiy, a suburb of Volgograd. I left Baku with three other poor conscripted souls, after waiting for three days at the station for the train to appear and transport us to our destination. Volzhskiy has its own colorful history, having been built by convict labor, each of whom received a house or an apartment after completing his prison sentence. The train was dirty and cold and there was no food. When we finally stopped at the southern Russian town of Tikhoretsk, we were fed a meal of *poltav kotlets* (boneless meat cutlets) and fried potatoes that to this day I remember as the tastiest I have ever eaten. We arrived in Volzhskiy several hours later, hungry again, dirty, and tired, and we stayed that way for the next six months.

Russian winters in general are fabled events, and many of those fables were written about winters in the Volgograd Oblast. The winter we were experiencing during my time there in 1974 to 1975 compared favorably to the winter that contributed to the defeat of the armies of the Third Reich. The cold was a separate life force with its own personality. I don't believe I regained any feeling in my toes until the spring thaw. Every day I had to unfold my fingers separately. I would watch my hand as each finger made its own independent decision to uncurl and renew its association with the rest of my body.

Breathing required thought. I could not do it voluntarily. I could only inhale with short staccato breaths, which made me dizzy, but long extended breathing was too painful. I couldn't decide if I was glad when the sun was shining or not. It offered some meager warmth, but the snow acted like a mirror and reflected the glare with such intensity that it rendered me blind, like when a photoflash goes off. Walking was an exercise in faith and hope that the ground in front of me was solid and flat. When I looked up, my eyes watered. The tears instantly froze on my cheeks, and my skin burned. The weather and the commanding officers shared the same sadistic sense of humor. My body temporarily warmed from the physical exertion of the military exercises, but as the exercises progressed, I would sweat so that my clothes stuck to my skin. It seemed that the commanding officers would watch and wait for those moments and then inexplicably abort the exercises and require us to stand at attention for who knew how long. As we stood there, our clothing froze and stiffened. I am shivering now as I write these words, remembering those days.

The sadistic antics of the officers were the only things that broke the monotony. Afternoons were filled with droning lectures regarding the technical aspects of warfare, and Communist propaganda films were the evening's entertainment. Lectures and films were interspersed with tasteless meals of harsh grain and *kotleti* (meatballs). We lived like monks in a silent order. Conversations consisted of Morse code–like blinks and stares transmitting warnings that an officer was approaching. There was no sense of friendship among the recruits; everyone was too busy dodging the next diatribe.

Powerlessness does not become me, so one night, not long after my beating, feverish and restless, I snuck out of the barracks and into the town. The barracks was a bleak two-story building with the sleeping area on the second floor. Lights had been out for about an hour. I was assigned a bed, a night table, and a small cupboard where I kept my toiletries, which were used only once a week when I was allowed to bathe. It had been another brutal day. Awakening at sunrise to a whooping alarm, we dressed quickly, packing our Kalashnikov rifles and ammunition, chemical masks and suits, and backpacks of additional fighting gear. The military base was located in a rural area near the Akhtyba, a tributary of the Volga, Europe's longest river, which forms the core of the largest river system in Europe.

We ran several miles down the hill to the frozen waters, crossed them, turned around, and ran back up a hill to the base, where we were served a lukewarm breakfast of *mannaya kasha* (similar to Cream of Wheat cereal or some other type of kasha or grain), hot tea in metal cups with two pieces of sugar, black bread, and butter. I had stopped counting my bruises and ignored every new pain and blister; it was a worthless exercise, which only made me unhappier. I was eighteen, and I missed my home. The youngest of four children, I was accustomed to the camaraderie of my brother and sisters. I enjoyed their attention and the extra care I garnered from my parents as the *sonbeshik* (the baby or youngest member of the group).

I listened for the steady breathing of my comrades as they each, having collapsed, fell into a heavy sleep. They slept inert, the sleep of the weary. I winced as my bed creaked while I shifted my pillow and blankets and molded them into the shape of a body. The cut under my eye was healing, and the bruise that had begun around the orb dripped down onto my cheek, leaving a serpentine river of yellow and purple in its wake. We slept in our clothes—a saving grace in the morning that allowed us an extra few precious minutes of sleep before we began the day.

My boots were on the left side of my bed, buffed to a high shine, per regulation. I held my breath, bent down, and pulled them on. I stood up slowly. A knifelike pain plunged through my side into my ribcage, a remnant of the kick I had received there. I closed my lips and bit down, touching my teeth to my tongue to keep from groaning. My cot was third from the door. Close. I walked toward it, careful to make no sound. Years of freezing winters and sultry summers had warped the door so that it scraped slightly as I opened it. Surprisingly, the hinge did not squeal. For some reason, as I moved the door toward me, a sort of suction effect occurred and wind blew in, making me shiver. A couple of men shifted in their beds; some pulled at their blankets, wrapping them tighter around their bodies. As I watched them move, I was sure someone would awaken. I didn't wait to find out; I hurried down the stairs and stepped outside.

I walked in the direction of the latrine, thinking if I were caught, I could easily explain my nighttime jaunt. No one stopped me, so I walked past it.

I am not sure what I hoped to find on my journey. I just followed my desire to disappear—at least for a while. I had been to the town before on leave: once to see a movie and once to visit a museum dedicated to the great victory. It was an easy walk toward the town along the paved two-lane road. The night was clear, and the glare from the moon lit my way. There wasn't much snow, but whatever water was in the air had crystallized onto the pavement, leading me on what seemed like an enchanted pathway. My walk was meditative; the quiet of the night surrounded my thoughts and drew them inward. I welcomed the freedom of walking without combat gear, listening only to my own footsteps. The road was deserted, so my view was uninterrupted by artificial light and structures. Under other circumstances, it might have been a lonely walk, but that night I welcomed the solitude. I looked up, and as many of us do, I wondered who else was gazing at the sky. I longed for home and my parents. I conjured their faces in my mind and began a conversation with them. I listened to the soothing sounds of my own breathing and felt the tension leave my shoulders.

Within fifteen minutes, I entered the outskirts of town. The dogs started to bark, and my mind flashed to World War II movies of frenzied animals ripping limbs off their victims. I picked up a large stick and looked down the street to see if any were coming after me. The wind shifted the shadows of the trees, and my stomach twisted from the rush of adrenaline. For the first time, I was immobilized with fear. I almost turned back, but some invisible force pushed me forward and guided me to one of the houses at the end of the street. As I think back, it really wasn't any different than any of the other houses on the street. There were no inviting lights, and although smoke billowed from the chimney, it billowed from every chimney in every home there. I could have spun myself around and randomly picked any house, but I picked that one. It was a lucky choice. It was a small two-story house with a tiled roof, dormered upstairs windows—really nothing out of the ordinary or particularly inviting, except perhaps there did not appear to be a dog. I knocked on the door, and a small, stooped man with gray, uncombed hair opened the door. His eyes were swollen with wrinkles, yet somehow he emitted youth and energy.

"Come inside, son."

I hesitated, still unsure I had made a safe choice.

"It is cold outside."

His face had deep wrinkles. His hands were profoundly veined and his long fingernails thick and yellowed. I don't think he had gone to bed yet because he was wearing light work pants and a button-down flannel shirt. I looked at him, and then beyond him into the house, took a deep breath, thanked him, and stepped in. The house had a pungent smoky smell that triggered some forgotten memory from my childhood. A rush of warmth and familiarity filled my heart. The man took my hand and led me to the main room, guiding me to a chair near the *pechka*. A Russian pechka is unlike an American fireplace. In small Russian towns during the winter months, the pechka is the traditional center of family life. It is huge and not only serves to heat the house and cook the food, but also, with the proper materials, it is used as a bed. It reminded me of the pechka at my grandparents' home in Shusha. I stared into the fire for a while and did not speak. The silence was warm, and I retreated to the safety of my memories.

Shusha was my childhood summer playground. Both of my parents were teachers; my father taught biology and chemistry and my mother taught Azeri and literature. They were born in Shusha, and every summer all six of us—my parents, my two sisters, my brother, and I—would travel eight hours by bus to Shusha along the long spiral mountain route and live in my grandfather's large hundred-year-old home. My memory has transformed the house into a castle. It was adorned with two large gated entrances leading to the main house down a stone road. There was a long wooden staircase in the center of the home that led to a balcony on the second floor. Three rooms issued from the balcony: the *zal* ("big room" in Azeri) was designed to receive guests; a second room, the *shushaband* (glass room), was a large windowed room designed specifically to capture the afternoon sun; and the third was a bedroom. Mulberry, or tut, trees paid homage to an old stone we used as a bench in the middle of the yard. The web of twigs and branches made for perfect climbing. I spent hours cradled in the shade, eating what I still believe to be the sweetest fruit on earth.

On cold nights I would drink tea from a big samovar, a special tea set for making tea on coal. I loved the smell of the burning coal; it embraced me and rocked me into the peaceful sleep of a child. From the stories of my parents and relatives, my grandfather looms large in my memory. He was the king of the castle and of course seemed ancient to me, but I remember him as a man of great courage and character. He was a wealthy businessman, who went by the nickname *Gizil Mukhtar* or Gold Mukhtar. He was big and strong, and the family legend is that he insisted on carrying the water buckets into the house each day and would accept no offer of help. There was no running water in the house, and as head of his home, he maintained it was his responsibility alone to provide it. Then one day after filling the buckets with water, he quietly lay down and died at the well.

Shusha was the soul of Azerbaijan. Artistry and inspiration grew out of its glacial lakes and lush green forests, planted by the hands of God. It was the home of dozens of poets, philosophers, musicians, authors, painters, and playwrights. *Shusha* means "glass" in Azeri, a reference to its crystal-like air. It served as a major resort destination within the former USSR from the 1960s through the 1980s. Its thousand-foot cliffs earned it the nickname "Soviet Switzerland." I remember it particularly for its stone streets and graceful mosques.

As a child, I would climb the mountain with my father and bathe in the natural mineral springs there. There were several routes up to the top. The level of difficulty of the climb was reflected in the Azeri names of the route traveled: the *eshshak yolu* was the "donkey road," which described the method of transportation used on that path; the *pishik yolu* was the "cat's road," which required astute climbing skills; and then there was the *girkh pilakan* or "forty stairs."

I watched the fire that night in that man's home in the village of Volzhskiy, town of Volgograd Oblast, and dreamed of Shusha. Then it was only the youthful heartache of a homesick boy, but today my dreams of Shusha are filled with the agony of knowing that the Shusha of my youth is in ruins, eviscerated by hatred and war. Memories are like fairy tales. Behind the beauty of the story hides the ugliness of the truth. The flames of the fire that night illuminated only my dreams of Shusha. The nightmares remained imprisoned in the darkness.

Throughout its history, Shusha experienced tensions between its ethnic Armenian and Azerbaijani residents. Shusha is a strategically located town on the top of the hill and the historical capital of the disputed Nagorno-Karabakh region, which was claimed by both the republics of Armenia and Azerbaijan.

Shusha has been recently liberated by the Azerbaijani army along with other parts of Nagorno-Karabakh as well as additional regions of Azerbaijan as a result of military operations, which started on September 27, 2020. The trilateral peace deal—signed by Azerbaijan, Armenia, and Russia on November 10, 2020—has effectively ended almost three decades of the occupation of the Azerbaijani territories by the Armenian forces.[5] The Russian peacekeeping forces were deployed to the area, and the joint Russian-Turkish monitoring centers will be established to observe the cease-fire. The outcome of this recent war and the terms of the peace deal have drastically redrawn the geopolitical map of the region. It is inevitably going to affect the role of other regional and global powers in the South Caucasus and the entire post-Soviet space as well as the role of international organizations such as the Organization for Security and Cooperation in Europe (OSCE), which proved to be ineffective in finding the solution to this centuries' old conflict and other conflicts in the post–Soviet and post–Warsaw Pact space. This artificially created territorial problem by the Russian empire in the last centuries, then maintained by Soviet leadership as leverage over both the Azerbaijani and Armenian people, has always led to tension and bloodshed throughout history.

There were outbursts of ethnic strife throughout my childhood as well. I remember my parents helping clean up a neighbor beaten in an attack, and we were caught in the middle of a deadly skirmish on our way to Isa bulaghi, a beautiful park with natural springs named after Isa.[6] I even became embroiled in a fistfight after being teased about my heritage. As a little boy, I spent every hour of every day up in the tut tree dreaming of all the things little boys dream about and watching my neighbors go about their day. One neighbor, Bahram, a big kid, maybe a year or two older than me, blessed with a muscular frame and impressed by it too, called at me from below. He insisted I was an Armenian eating fruit from trees that only ethnic Azerbaijanis should enjoy.

I hope I was not offended by the misidentification but rather by the obvious intent to insult me; however, I was only a child, and the truth is, I probably understood even then that an Azerbaijani of any character would not tolerate being referred to as Armenian. In contrast to Bahram, I was small and skinny, but I refused to acknowledge that disadvantage. I was insulted and intended to avenge my honor and the honor of my people. So,

I waited for an opportune moment, and one day, as I was returning from the *torpag meydani* or the ground square,[7] having purchased a loaf of bread per my mother's instructions, I came upon Bahram. I sucker-punched him and gave him a bloody nose. As is true of many boys and of too many men, a show of force earns respect, and Bahram and I later became best friends.

The Soviet quarantine on all things ethnic and religious actually kept conflicts between the Armenians and the Azerbaijanis in check, but once the stranglehold of Communism was lifted and the former satellite countries claimed independence, the conflicts boiled to the surface. During the late 1980s, as the politicians pretended to talk peace, the Nagorno-Karabakh conflict exploded, and the Armenian army captured Shusha.

My sister, uncles, aunts, and cousins all lived in Shusha at the time. They were told if they did not leave, they would be murdered. Almost the entire ethnic Azerbaijani population fled, numbering in the tens of thousands. My sister told me they were shocked by the sudden onslaught of the Armenian forces. There was no real Azerbaijani resistance, which made her believe there was some sort of payoff to the Azerbaijani military. All of a sudden, Shusha was surrounded from all directions.

A similar situation took place with other towns of Nagorno-Karabakh at the time, such as Khojaly, which was blocked on three sides. The storm of the city began with a two-hour artillery bombardment, which was conducted by tanks, armored vehicles, and guns, with the Alazan missiles, Grad and Uragan installations, and military equipment of the 366th Motorized Rifle Regiment of the former Soviet Army. The military personnel of the Russian army's 366th regiment took an active part in the storming of Khojaly. Those events became known as the Khojaly massacre. The *Jerusalem Post* wrote that the Khojaly massacre, which was committed with incredible brutality, was one of the worst tragedies of the twentieth century. In Shusha, my sister, her family, and the rest of my extended family left with only the things they could carry. Even their refrigerators remained stocked with food. My grandfather's home was confiscated by Armenians, some of whom may have been refugees driven from their homes by Azerbaijanis. Many still live in the refugee camps created after the siege. They fester there with little electricity and no running water, awaiting their professed right of return. And the Armenians remained in the rubble of collapsed roofs, broken walls, and windowless homes. There was no money to invest in rebuilding. The mosques are covered with graffiti, and the springs are surrounded by waste and weeds. There were no Azerbaijanis living in Shusha until today, and you could only enter the region from Armenia. There was no compromise, and positions over the last decades have hardened; both parties wanted the same piece of decimated land and refused to share it with the other. In the meantime, Shusha no longer hosted concerts and dance recitals. It didn't inspire artists and poets for almost three decades. The residents subsisted on government handouts and whatever else they could eke out on this land. And when there was nothing else, they filled their bellies with the satisfaction of revenge. It seems to me there are just a finite number of stories in the world. Locations change and character traits are added or subtracted, but in the end, it's all the same. I mean, how many stories are there really? Stories about love lost, infidelity, corrupting power, altruism and sainthood, struggle and redemption. It seems to me, as I sit here and remember that pechka and the pechka of my grandparents, the stories all seem to intertwine.

There had been no direct light when I was standing at the entrance of that man's home outside of Volzhskiy. All he saw at that time was the featureless form of a shivering boy in combat fatigues, but the light from the fire illuminated my face. Recognition reflected in his eyes when he noticed my bruise, but he said nothing. I looked around. The room was small and comfortable: dark wood floors, white walls, simple curtains, and cushioned chairs. At some point during those quiet moments, his wife entered the room. She looked at me, and sympathy crossed her face. She glanced at her husband, and it seemed to me that they were silently conducting a conversation. The man pulled a chair up next to mine and took my hand into both of his. He gazed so earnestly into my eyes that I felt compelled to turn mine away.

"What is your name, son?"

"Mahir," I answered and met his eyes again.

"Where are you from?"

"Baku . . . Azerbaijan," I added, unsure if he knew where Baku was.

"Ah, far from your home."

He continued to ask me simple questions, the kind you ask when you first meet someone and are trying to learn enough information to continue the conversation. I hadn't noticed that his wife had left the room.

"Are you in trouble?"

I said I was not but that I was sick, and I missed home. A young woman, who I later learned was the man's daughter, perhaps a little older than I and apparently awakened by our conversation, came into the room. She was wearing a faded nightgown and slippers and held a crocheted shawl tight around her shoulders. She stood behind her father for a minute. Our eyes met briefly, and then she turned and quietly walked out. She returned with her mother and handed me a bowl filled with hot *shee*, Russian soup made with beef broth and cabbage. The daughter brought a chair over, so that her mother could sit next to her father, and then took her place again behind him. I finished the soup quickly, and the wife stood and took the bowl from me. She offered me a second helping that I refused, but I agreed to a cup of tea, which the daughter delivered from the kitchen. Finally, warm and comfortable, I told them about the beating I had endured days earlier.

"You must be careful not to anger the officers. Just do as you are told; it will be over soon," the old man said.

Finally, the daughter, too, pulled up a chair, and we all talked about ourselves and our lives. I am afraid I did most of the talking, because I learned little about them except that the daughter had been married to an abusive man. She was very sweet and, like many creatures of the north, she sported an extra layer or two of heat-retaining body insulation. She smiled often, patted my knee, and laughed at the slightest provocation. The mother, identical to the daughter in stature and frankly not much older looking, reacted in much the same way as her daughter. In short, it was obvious the family saw me as a potential son-in-law. I was warm and full-bellied, and I am sure I wasn't as forthright as I should have been in discouraging them, but I was sincerely grateful for their kindness. I spent a long time talking to them, eating, and generally rebuilding my faith in the human race. I left several hours later, laden with food and good wishes, and changed somehow. I saw the man and his family only one other time: on May 9, Victory Day, my unit, dressed in formal uniform, paraded down the central street as part of the festivities celebrating the defeat of the Germans in the Second World War. Although the locals clearly didn't need any encouragement, they used the holiday as an excuse to bring out the vodka and beer.

Many of the unmarried young girls in the town were taking photographs with the soldiers, and the daughter sought me out to take a picture with her.

* * * * *

As I took my oath of citizenship pledging allegiance to the United States, I remembered my walk back to the base that night some thirty years earlier. I returned to camp early the next morning, was found out and punished, but I survived. Since my act of defiance did not kill me, I began to believe that I might have the power to control my own destiny.

As the train pulled out of the station away from Volgograd moving west, we did not seek comfort among one another; instead, we clung to each other out of fear—fear of each other and the West, that unknown behemoth that sought to destroy us: the jewel that was the great Soviet Union. Ignorance was the essential glutinous ingredient. Truth and education were the only antidotes, but they had to be delivered carefully or they would be manipulated and distorted and serve as further strengthening compounds. The friendship and shared purpose between young US soldiers were an anathema to the Soviet soldier and, now I think also, to the Iraqi soldier, although not to the Iraqi insurgent whose religious or ideological affiliation are seemingly impenetrable.

We gathered strength from the knowledge that we had survived basic training and were on our way to complete our required army service. For the next eighteen months, I was stationed in Kaliningrad, the most western point of the former Soviet Union and the present Russian Federation, situated on the shores of the Baltic Sea and bordered by Poland and Lithuania. I spent quite a bit of time in or on the Baltic Sea, pulling pontoon bridges from one piece of land to another or driving armored personnel carriers through the water. Fortunately, the weather in Kaliningrad was much more temperate than in my previous deployment, so although I hated standing in the water, the experience was not nearly as painful as a cadet during my basic training in the region of Volgograd Oblast.

We arrived at Kaliningrad station to shouts of "Molodiye prishli, molodiye prishli!" ("youngsters" have arrived or "new blood" has arrived in Russian). The *dembels* (graduates) were leaving; we would be the newest victims. Perhaps it was the *banyas* (bathhouses) in the city that were guarded and maintained by the soldiers for the use and enjoyment of senior Soviet generals, for although the officers in Kaliningrad were not kind and caring men, they were not the brutes of Volgograd. Indeed, our field commander, a Lithuanian, was a good man who kept the troops organized and out of harm's way.

The Kaliningrad region served as a bridge between the east and west and has a somewhat schizophrenic feel to it. Shopkeepers sell Nazi-era paraphernalia alongside Soviet iconography. After World War II, the Soviet Union annexed this former German territory, which used to be a northern part of Eastern Prussia with the center in Konigsberg, and waged a campaign to erase all evidence of German culture. The territory has been renamed the Kaliningrad Oblast or region, and the former capital Konigsberg has become the city of Kaliningrad. An ethnically German miller recounted a story to me of being forced to watch as Soviet soldiers raped his daughter. He was very old, and his bodily decay mirrored the decay of the city. He whistled as he spoke through broken teeth, wishing me good health and a long and prosperous life. He had witnessed Nazi atrocities too. None are blameless. He remained in the town of his birth and raised his family. I fell in love with his granddaughter for an evening as we sorted the grain and worked the machines, and I relaxed in the monotony of simple farm work. He was satisfied with his decision to remain in his ancestral home. Many years later, I would take the opposite road and leave mine. It is only now that I live in the United States that I understand his attachment to the place. The outskirts of what is left of the town are filled with disintegrating farmhouses built by the Germans and poorly functioning Soviet collective farms. I heard a rumor that skeletons of Nazi soldiers remain unburied on a secluded beach, and another that a bridge that had been destroyed or kept open by the Nazi troops as they retreated remained in that condition, apparently immune to all attempts to repair it or close it back to make it functional. There is very little to do in Kaliningrad; alcoholism is the local hobby, and sex is easy and plentiful. During the eighteen months I spent there, several dozen soldiers disappeared into the bowels of a local hospital. No official explanation was offered, but I later learned that the soldiers had contracted syphilis.

Ever mindful of its image, the army ignored the epidemic, treated the symptoms, and sent the soldiers away, uneducated, to infect other parts of the population. My commanding officer, Captain Butakov, was one of the very few good men I met in the army. It took him very little time, after having learned about my release from the army, to inform me of the good news. I yelped with joy; it had been two very long years since I had been home. There was no one to say goodbye to, no addresses to exchange, but I had been deeply affected by my experiences, and my life was about to alter course.

2

The Search for Identity

The roles of mother and child had reversed. First it was a young boy peering out behind the curtains awaiting the return of the mother. Later it was his mother looking out onto the roads surrounding the *microrayon* (from Russian meaning "micro district," a large-scale residential complex) waiting for her son. The microrayon was the architectural symbol of the Soviet system. Nicknamed *Khrushchevki* to honor Nikita Khrushchev, they were prolific concrete-building complexes that mushroomed across the entire Soviet space during the early 1960s. The microrayons were massive prefabricated neighborhoods devoid of imagination and creativity. There is no art or beauty in Soviet architecture—only function. Design and beauty had its place but not in the ordinary working lives of citizens. Natural obstacles were used as barriers between neighborhoods, which were designed to perform as self-contained units that included schools, stores, playgrounds, and maintenance units.

Every day during my last month of deployment, my mother would look out upon the ugly uniform landscape. It was the second such complex she had lived in during her married life. The first was located in a volatile sector of Baku called Sovietski ("Soviet" in Russian), which was populated with thugs and thieves. The second complex was safer but no more visually appealing. She watched for my return, worried about her youngest son, remembering her eldest daughter who had died during childhood. She knew she could not survive such a loss again. She recalled watching me play with my older siblings in the snow and eating sweets during *Nowruz*, a March holiday celebrating the beginning of spring. She had waited the same way for their father; however, she was forced to wait for him for six long years. He finally returned from World War II, which was the Great Patriotic War for the Soviets, but he had suffered an injury. He was never the same after that. My father was a good man with great integrity, and I have fond memories of spending hours walking around the city of Baku with him. At the time, Baku was a city that embraced many diverse religions and ethnicities. I would sit with him on the shores of the Caspian Sea, listen to the sirens of incoming and departing ships, and breathe in the wet, salty air, unaware of the future conflicts that awaited the city and the ethnic strife that would rip the fabric of its multicultural society. On Saturdays, my father would take me to the *hamam* (traditional Azeri bathhouses). He would stay in for a half hour or more; I could not tolerate the heat for more than five minutes. In the outer room, we would be served tea with sugar in traditional Azeri fashion: the tea was bitter, so you would bite the sugar and keep it in your mouth while you sipped the liquid. When we arrived home, my mother, who had been cooking all day, would serve a feast of *khingal* (boiled wheat and meat topped with garlic-spiced yogurt) and *shirin ash* (sweet pilaf from Azeri), and rice mixed with meat, fruits, and vegetables. In public, my father maintained his composure, even withstanding an assault by a drugged-out patron of the bathhouse. But my father was easily angered at home and would seek relief in the same medicine many Soviets relied on: vodka. When he did, he became aggressive. My brother and I would be forced to withstand his tirades while my sister scuttled my mother to the safety of a room out of reach from my father's fists. It didn't happen often, but when it did, my sisters, my brother, and I all learned how to protect ourselves very early in life. I arrived back in Baku by train, having traveled through Rostov, one of the oldest towns in Russia. The train station in Rostov was filled with soldiers, drunken men, and gypsies. I noticed a pair of gypsies, a mother with her young daughter, and asked the mother to read my palm. As she did, her face dropped, and she refused to look up. She quickly told me something I no longer remember; I knew it was not what she had seen. I continue to wonder if whatever it was she saw still lies ahead of me. No one knew about my return. I ran to my home and opened the door. My father was sitting at the kitchen table drinking tea. He looked up, expecting my brother, saw me, and began to sob. I cried too. He came to me and grabbed me into a bear hug. We stood for a while, wrapped in each other's arms. I buried my head in his neck and inhaled the sweet smell of familiarity. My brother, still living at home, returned a short while later. He hugged me too, then pulled off my shirt and commented on my well-toned body, making me feel for the first time I was his equal and a man. My brother took me to my mother, who was still teaching at a nearby elementary school. We entered the classroom, and the children saw me first. She followed their eyes; it took her a moment to process her vision. Then she too burst into tears and ran into my arms. The children were young and confused, and they all began to wail.

So, I began to laugh, my brother laughed, and my mother, not knowing what to do, broke into hiccups. For the next few minutes, it was complete pandemonium, with children and adults alternating between laughter and tears. After a few days' rest, I returned to the studies I had left, but it was not the same. When I think about how I got to where I am from where I was, I have come to believe I am programmed to reconfigure disappointments into challenges. As a young man with no political connections and even less money to bribe officials, I wasn't expected to pursue higher education. Expectations be damned, I wanted to be a doctor. Despite clear evidence that I was doomed to defeat, I applied for entry into the medical school at Baku State University—ENTRY DENIED. As a child, I had scaled the walls of my summer camp because I did not like the boundaries they created between me and whatever place I wanted to go. As a young adult, I bristled at the boundaries of graft and nepotism that kept me from whatever future I chose to pursue.

Entry into the medical school had been denied, but it was like a maze. There was another route available. I could enter and graduate from the technical dentistry program of the Baku medical college and from there leapfrog to the state institute. Entry into the technical dentistry program was highly competitive and bribes greased the way for many students, but not all. So I hit the books. I studied through three months of a stultifying summer and aced the entrance exam. I am sure someone could have dreamed up some pretext to keep me from the program, but it must have been too much work, because I was granted admission. I initially began school in September 1974 and, at the time, I made two new best friends: Eldar, a tall handsome fellow who hobbled due to an amputated leg but was supported and loved by his childhood sweetheart, and Alesha, an ethnic Armenian of great character and integrity. Their approach to learning was very practical: they were in school to learn how to make teeth so that they could then earn a lot of money. I was the most esoteric of the group and found myself drawn to all of the nontechnical classes. In November 1974, I was called upon to join the Soviet army. After my return from the army in November 1976, I continued my studies in the technical dentistry program of the Baku medical college.

When I started school again in 1976, I renewed my friendships with Eldar and Alesha, but they were not the same; they had already graduated by then and were busy with their jobs and families. The building I had studied in two years before had been renovated. The new building was more modern now but still built in the sterile communist style. I sat in a backless chair with a round seat (I think it was green plastic) with two pairs of aluminum legs that seemed to either grow or shorten overnight. The counter I worked on top of was white, and the lights under which I worked were florescent. Eldar and Alesha would often come to our cafeteria, and we lunched together. It was a big room, simply designed, consisting of wood tables and small plastic chairs. I remember two big windows with curtains, and in the summertime, we had a lot of light coming in through those windows, which I liked very much. Sometimes we went to downtown Baku. Many years later, ethnic issues would bring a lot of suffering and death, but then we could go to the boulevard across the central *Neftchilar prospecti* ("Oilmen Avenue" in Azeri), pass the maiden tower, G*is galasi* (in Azeri), and see Russians, Armenians, Jews, and others walking along the Caspian Sea, enjoying the fresh air and beautiful view together. Everybody proudly referred to themselves as *Bakintsi* ("Bakuvians" in Russian) regardless of their ethnicity. I remember the oil smell of the boulevard and the sirens of incoming and departing ships. It was wonderful but temporary. Many years later, politicians would destroy everything for the sake of their ambitions and political games.

Despite my experiences with the army system, I remained a dedicated Communist. I was voted Komsomol—leader of the Communist youth organization in the dentistry program—which required me to organize various community-service activities consistent with the Communist ideology of unity. In truth, the planned activities were more like slave labor. In the summer of 1976, we were sent to the Barda area of Azerbaijan, an agricultural community located west of Baku, to help the farmers there. We lived in a dirty warehouse full of rats, which was bad enough, but more infuriating was the special treatment one of my colleagues was receiving. He was the son of a highly placed official in the Communist Party. He was not required to sleep in the warehouse and dined with the leaders of the program. At the time, I refused to believe this unequal treatment was the result of deficiencies in the system; I believed it was a singular, unrelated event. Later, when it was time to graduate, I would again be victimized by the inherent inequities of Communism and the system of graft and corruption upon which its foundation lay. I was an A student. By every standard of measure, I deserved to graduate summa cum laude. The problem was, the institution was awarded only a set number of such diplomas, and they were for sale to the highest bidder. My family was not poor, but we did not have extra cash to pay for bribes. I learned I was not scheduled to receive the honors diploma I deserved, and I was livid. I met with several administrators of the school and pleaded my case. The administrators were forced to acknowledge their "mistake," and I was ultimately awarded the sought-after diploma. Rather than awaken me to the knowledge that the system was corrupt, my success combined with my youth and naïveté served to reinforce my belief that the problem lay with various individuals and not with Communism.

Of course, life was not all work and patriotic party duty. Although the architecture of Communism was ugly, its women most certainly were not, and I did my fair share of investigating their structural details. My most memorable dalliance was with Gamar, a very beautiful woman several years older than me who worked as an administrator of the dentistry program. Gamar was a very persistent young woman. Unfortunately, my mother did not like her and screened all calls from her, finally causing a confrontation between us where I was forced to tell Gamar our relationship could not move forward. It was not only my mother's disapproval of Gamar that kept the relationship from growing—I was bored, and the tedium of my life infected my desire to pursue a serious romance. I graduated with my summa cum laude diploma and set out to find a job. Predictably, that too required connections or money to pay bribes, which I still did not possess. I do, however, possess a great deal of luck. It turned out the director of the local clinic was a man with the last name of Ibrahimov. We were not related, but he apparently liked his name and therefore liked me. The female comrade who happened to be the director of the medical clinic took a liking to me too—which I was happy to encourage—and she persuaded Mr. Ibrahimov to hire me. She also convinced him that I was only planning to work in the clinic for a short time, which was important, since it meant he would sooner be able to collect a bribe for the next man's employment. It later became clear to me that Mr. Ibrahimov's main occupation was collecting bribes and sharing the profits with his superiors. In fact, at the time, I think I was the only person who was hired at Central Clinic #5 in Baku without having to pay a bribe. It was a good deal for Mr. Ibrahimov and his colleagues. I am a hard worker, and production levels rose during my tenure, making him look good. I was also awarded the first Communist Party membership position ever offered to the clinic. It was a huge status boost for the clinic, earning it the right of representation, which could later lead to additional cash or the opportunity to be among the first to receive equipment or upgrades, or both. It was a small victory for all of us "ordinary," unconnected folks. All of the directors believed the membership would be awarded to one of the dentists, who held a higher status than the technicians. After a general meeting of all of the employees of the clinic and speeches made by all of the candidates, I won the vote. The corruption in the system still existed, but this time it was defeated. The clinic was located in a gray, single-story building with few windows. To the right from the entrance of the clinic there were several doctors' offices that served various dental professionals. The technicians' laboratory was a big room with equipment that was quite primitive, taking into consideration that it was the 1970s and imports of the more sophisticated Western equipment were very limited. The room was usually hot and overcrowded with technicians, and the long corridor was always full of patients sitting and waiting. In an attempt to add some style to the space, somebody with a very poor artistic eye placed blue and white paintings on the walls. I worked in the clinic for two long years. I was paid a good wage, but the comfort the money provided was not enough to make me happy. Some may call it artistry, but those would be people without talent or imagination. Creating teeth, even those made of gold, is about as exciting as watching paint dry. Every Monday, I met my friends for lunch; every

Saturday, I played soccer. The clinic was located near the Avrora metro station in a very polluted part of Baku called *Cherniy gorod* (black city), a reference to the poor air. I lived in my parents' home and traveled to the clinic by overcrowded bus.

As terrible as my time in the army was, it was the first time I had traveled outside of my country, and it was exciting. When I listened for the sounds of my life back in Baku, I heard nothing but white noise. One day, like the cartoon light bulb that bursts into view, a thought suddenly occurred to me: I didn't want to be a technical dentist. I wanted to be an international journalist. I didn't know any journalists at the time, national or international, so I am not sure how I developed the idea. True, I could speak Azeri and Russian, but that wouldn't get me very far. The title "international journalist" promised travel and even hinted at intrigue, and it clearly was a whole lot more interesting than making teeth. I began to write for small local publications and took several classes in English. I discovered I had a gift for languages, progressed quickly through my classes, and within two years I was speaking English fluently. Single-mindedness is the pleasure of youth; I drove toward the vision of my future and accepted no lure or detour. But I have heard it said that while man plans, God laughs. Despite my ambition, my plans to find my destiny were almost derailed.

Sometime in the early morning hours of June 6, 1979, my mother entered the room I shared with my brother. She gently shook me out of my slumber, and then shocked me into consciousness with a whisper:

"Your father is ill. He is dying."

My father was not an old man; he was the picture of health just hours before. I ran from my room and crossed the hall into my parents' bedroom. Whatever had happened during the hours I was asleep convinced my mother that my father needed medical attention. I pushed through the strange bodies in white costumes floating around his bed. They were moving slowly, placing blankets on top of my father's prone body. His eyes were closed, but his chest was moving. Then, unbelievably, the medical team stepped away from his bedside and began to file out the door. I accosted one of them.

"Where are you going? Stay here!"

The nurse looked at me and then at my mother who was standing next to me. My mother took my elbow and guided me back to the bed where my father lay; his eyes were still closed, and his breathing was shallow. I stared at his face, which was unnaturally gray, the color of stone; his lips were thin and blue. It was only minutes later that I witnessed his death rattle. My father emitted a whooping rasp and then silence.

I had been scheduled to leave the next morning for the Moscow State Institute of International Relations to begin my studies. Career change in a communist state is no simple task. Unlike in the United States, I couldn't just leave my position and start anew. In order to begin my new studies, I had to apply first to the government for permission to take an aptitude exam. The Soviet educational system is completely alien to US custom and tradition.

As with everything else Soviet, continuing education in certain elite institutions required state approval. Without it, I would not be even given the opportunity to take the entry exams in one of those institutions. And, if approved and accepted, I was considered a representative of the Soviet Republic of Azerbaijan and was expected to fulfill my international duty to my country—in other words, do well and stay out of trouble. I had completed my interview months before with each of the state officials and party bosses, and they gave me permission to travel to Moscow as a representative of Azerbaijan. I had done so and met with the Moscow officials of the institute, who then approved my application to take the aptitude exam. I took the exam, and I passed. I was scheduled to begin my studies when my father died. I was grief-stricken by my loss and began to lose faith in myself.

Death is so small; the person is here and then they are not. But the empty space in which I lived after my father died was cavernous. I found comfort in old religious customs that my family had ceased to practice for generations. It gave me a tool to process my grief. Prior to 1920, when the Russian Bolshevik army invaded, a majority of Azerbaijanis were practicing Shi'a Muslims. However, during the Soviet regime, religious practices were systematically repressed, and Azerbaijanis, like much of the Soviet population, simply stopped practicing them. I was then, and remain, a secular Muslim, but I am thankful for the sense of calm the funeral preparations required.

According to religious law, my father's body had to be cleansed and then quickly buried so that his soul could rest. The reality of my father's death came to me through the touch of my fingers on his skin as my brother and I washed his body with scented water. A body without life is cold; it moves as a single block with odd parts attached by heavy hinges. It is at the same time pliable and resistant, but its resistance is by weight instead of force. Moving him and holding his body was like molding a pliable piece of lead.

Someone, I am not sure who, purchased the traditional white *kafan* (white cotton or linen cloth) in which my brother and I wrapped our father. He was buried in Muslim tradition without a coffin in an area close to our home, a place I have not been to in a long time but still visit in my dreams. I relived my father's death countless times in Iraq. I hope it made me more sensitive to the needs of the men and families I served there. I spent the next year in Baku healing my wounds and coming to terms with my father's passing. Finally, the next year, I gathered my courage and, in homage to my father, I once again embraced my dream. I was given permission to take exams at the Peoples' Friendship University of Russia to study international law. Upon arriving in Moscow, I was asked to interview and take proficiency exams for the newly created international journalism program. Again, I passed and was offered a spot in the new program. It was my dream becoming reality. I was sure I was being given a gift from my father, who I felt was watching over me and guiding me through my new life. The majority of the students in the program were from countries outside of the Soviet Union: Asia, Africa, and South America. I lived in the *obshejitie* ("university dormitory" in Russian). My first roommate was a very wealthy man from Kuwait and my second, Alexander, was from Byelorussia. Alex was tall, handsome, and shy. He was the perfect lure for young women. He often brought them into the dorm, but they spent the night with me. Needless to say, I have very fond memories of my escapades with my roommate and friend.

The course of study was rigorous. First-year Soviet students were required to become fluent in two languages other than their native tongue. I was selected to study Arabic and English. Non-Soviets were required to study Russian. The rest of the curriculum included coursework in history, literature, and domestic and international journalism. Also required was a steady dose of Communist propaganda. We were each required to attend meetings of the Komsomol, the Soviet youth organization, as well as meetings of the Communist Party committee at the university. In 1986, I was awarded a master of arts in international journalism and linguistics, and thereafter a PhD from the Academy of Social Sciences in Moscow. By the time I had completed my studies in 1991, I spoke five languages fluently: Azeri, Russian, English, Arabic, and Turkish. Given the chance, I could travel the world; getting the chance was another story entirely. I am single-minded to a fault. I worked tirelessly on my studies almost to the exclusion of all else. My academic achievements were hard to ignore. Other than eventually being awarded my degree summa cum laude, the recognition I received was in the form of jibes and insults from ethnic Russians, and the privileges I was granted were fewer than those granted to classmates with weaker grades but stronger connections to the party elite and more money to spend on administrators and teachers. The deeply held racist beliefs of the ethnic Russians were only barely concealed during the Soviet reign, and upon its collapse, all pretense was dropped. During my schooling, I was frequently reminded of my ethnic heritage and in no uncertain terms told to keep my tongue and know my place. Even in gym class my teacher made it a point of telling me that all of the political and economic troubles of the time were the fault of my race—the Caucasians. I was a churka, from one of the Caucuses, and therefore a person of lesser status. The epithet hurled at me from the lips of the ugly granddaughter of a former Moscow Communist Party boss stung. She was a classmate of mine and given praise and privileges beyond her due. She was a mean-spirited girl who abused her position. What was most revealing was that her father was Armenian; however, she chose to deny that heritage in favor of her mother's pure Russian blood.

One of the few friendships I forged during my time at the university was with a professor by the name of Farid Shukurovich Alizadeh, who taught Farsi. He was an ethnic Azeri but had never lived in Azerbaijan. It was his lifelong dream to move back to his homeland. He was a gentle, intelligent man and did his best to raise his family in accordance with Azeri culture and tradition. He had a daughter a few years younger than I, and I know he wished we would marry. No culture has a monopoly on good children; there will always be some who try to harm their parents, but in the Soviet system, a child could use the government as a weapon against their family. Professor Alizadeh's daughter almost succeeded. She married a man who did not meet her family's approval and left Moscow. She later returned and attempted to convince the government that she should be awarded part of the property her father had worked decades to obtain. She was able to convince one of the party bosses to investigate her father's property. The boss was envious of the professor. Despite all the superior amenities he received as party boss, the apartment he had been awarded was only moderate in size. Professor Alizadeh's was larger. According to Soviet law, if the professor's apartment was larger than the party determined his needs were, his daughter could claim part of it for herself. Fortunately, she lost her bid, but I was deeply disturbed and angered by the story. Later, his son was brutally murdered, and the crime was never solved. The stress overwhelmed my dear professor, and he died of a heart attack shortly thereafter. Still, I remained blinded by the Communist rhetoric and believed with all my heart that my achievements would win me success; the problem was with individuals, not with the system.

The End of the Empire and the Soviet Experiment in Afghanistan

My father's death was quick and painless for him. The death of the Soviet Union was slow. It was marked by periods of deterioration, followed by short surges of power for the old communist leaders. Iraq, too, is suffering a long painful death. Former leaders and those who held privileged positions are fighting to retain their power. Of course, the details differ significantly, but the general story is the same. As the old regime dies, the coalition forces are playing midwife to the difficult birth of a new order. For me, it felt like déjà vu all over again.

In June 1986, I had begun working for the executive committee of the Red Cross for the USSR. I had a job typical of the communist era: I was assigned to the International Department of the Central Committee of the Communist Party, and it was my responsibility to use my language skills to review open and public information published by Western agencies regarding Soviet–American relations. I assessed the information and reported to the former USSR ambassador to the United States, Anatoly Dobrynin, and later to Valentin Falin, former Soviet ambassador to West Germany, as well as Dmitry Lisovolik, who headed up the US/Canada division of the department.

I met Nikolai at the Medvedkovo metro station in a suburb of Moscow in November 1988. Moscow still was the capital of an empire that was destined to collapse in just a few years. Nikolai was telling me about his past experiences in Afghanistan as a former *spetznaz* (Soviet special forces) member. Seven hundred members of this elite spetznaz, under the command of twenty-three-year-old Rustam Tursunkulov, stormed President Hafizullah Amen's palace in winter 1979. That marked the beginning of the ten-year Soviet invasion of Afghanistan. The reason for the invasion: the Soviets decided that the pro-Soviet Afghan president was not pro-Soviet enough.

Afghanistan once again became a battleground of empires. Many years later, I would be fascinated to learn from the BBC that Rustam, who now lives in Moscow, and a woman, who as a girl had survived the onslaught in the Afghan president's palace that lasted forty-three minutes, would be connected through video teleconferencing (VTC). More than thirty years later, she was asking Rustam difficult moral questions. Almost everybody in the palace was murdered that night as part of the former Soviet military doctrine, which ultimately led to more than one million Afghan deaths, destruction of the country, and loss of the hearts and minds of Afghans.

Nikolai is a huge, athletically built guy in a primitive wheelchair that he moves with his hands. He returned from Afghanistan after being ambushed by Afghan *mujahedeen* (holy warriors) and lost his legs. Despite his youth, he seemed completely lost and morally devastated. He blamed the West and China for the support of mujahedeen and the Afghans for the betrayal. He was telling me that many Afghans were calling them friends and brothers but then turned against them and joined the insurgency. He repeatedly asked what went wrong and why the "internationalist duty" of the Soviets was not appreciated and welcomed. He said that the country was making huge sacrifices: militarily, politically, and economically. Yet he still believed in the popular notion of the country that Afghanistan was going to become the sixteenth Soviet Republic of the USSR, and he still considered himself a proud Soviet citizen. "Nobody can defeat our country; our country is the greatest!" he proudly declared.

He showed me the brochure given to him and his comrades as a part of the Soviet counterinsurgency (COIN) tactics in Afghanistan. Many years later, I saw the equivalent of those materials with do's and don'ts disseminated to US troops being deployed to Iraq and Afghanistan. The brochure, published in 1987, contains prohibitions for Soviet troops serving in Afghanistan:

1. Do not enter into unsanctioned contacts.
2. Do not try to talk to local women.
3. Do not visit private stores or individuals to buy goods, alcoholic beverages, or drugs.
4. Do not accept any gifts from local officials or individuals.
5. Do not take your clothes off for sunbathing in front of locals.
6. Keep the secrecy while discussing military topics; be aware that many Afghans are fluent in Russian.

The country of which I was then a citizen no longer exists. The army in which I served, luckily before the Soviet invasion of Afghanistan, is also gone.

The accords of April 14, 1988, included the principles of noninterference and nonintervention, the voluntary return of Afghan refugees, and interrelationships for settling the situation. The phased withdrawal of foreign troops was supposed to begin on May 15. The United States and the USSR also signed a declaration of international guarantees, stating they would both refrain from any form of interference and intervention. In the first three months, it was reported that some 50,183 foreign troops had withdrawn, with another 50,100 withdrawn between August 15, 1988, and February 15, 1989. During the withdrawal, troop convoys came under attack by Afghan fighters, and seventy-two Soviets were killed. The total withdrawal of all Soviet troops from Afghanistan was completed on February 15, 1989. In a symbolic move, Lieutenant General Boris Gromov, commander of the Soviet contingent in Afghanistan, was the last to leave the country.

I remember the TV images when Gromov turned for the last time toward Afghan territory and walked away. He was the last Soviet soldier to walk from Afghanistan back into Soviet territory. These images of the Soviet troops withdrawing from Afghanistan over the bridge to the former Soviet Central Asian Republic still live in my memory.[1]

3

The Disappearing Empire

Cultural, Ethical, and Geopolitical Implications

"A Look into the Soul"

A strange incident took place in the second part of the 1980s that remains a mystery until today. It seems to me that I met somebody whose soul I deeply sensed. Although this isolated incident might not seem to be important, my feeling is that it was one of the signs of many upcoming tragedies that would follow the collapsing Soviet empire in just a few years. The unexpected demise of a big system, similar to other big empires across history, had created a huge geopolitical vacuum and led to many casualties and atrocities across the entire post-Soviet, post–Warsaw Pact space, the Middle East, Southwest Asia, and the Western Hemisphere, as well as other parts of the world. Mikhail Gorbachev's reforms had set into motion changes that not everybody was prepared for. As a direct result of the lost socialist or Communist ideology, people were searching for and trying to find a new sense of or meaning of life. Belief in God, which was taken away from them with the Bolshevik revolution after 1917, was returning to the minds and hearts of the people, and later, under President Vladimir Putin, God would once again become an ideological tool of the Russian government combined with Russian patriotic nationalism based on socioculture and history, which forms the Russian mindset. These quickly changing realities led many unprepared people toward moral and identity crises. That's why I call this incident "a look into the soul."

This is a short story about the fate and moral crisis of a person I met in the final days of the collapse of the former USSR. Additionally, the experiences of meeting Soviet soldiers returning from Afghanistan coupled with this particular person's life experience prompted me to reconsider my own personal life and its meaning.

The incident took place in 1986, one year after Mikhail Sergeyevich Gorbachev, the eighth and last leader of the Soviet Union, came to power and started his reforms. That day, the Russian Orthodox Yelokhovo Church, the largest open church in Moscow, was crowded. Although there were many other young people in the church, she immediately attracted my attention. She was praying along with other worshipers during the Christmas midnight mass led by a patriarch. I came closer. She was very pretty, with light-colored hair and blue eyes. She was probably not older than nineteen. What surprised me was her honesty, passion, and especially the sadness in her eyes despite her young age. Although I was standing very close to her, trying to understand her world, she seemed to be so deeply involved in her own internal known world that it was very obvious that she was not paying attention to anything or anybody around her. The bright and powerful light, which her eyes reflected during the service, made me very uncomfortable and, at the same time, even a little frightened, causing a sense of curiosity.

The service was finally over. She lit the candle, wrapped her head in a woolen shawl, and left the church along with others. A sense of curiosity combined with desire and some invisible force led me to follow her. I wanted to understand her secret, fully appreciate her world and feelings that made her so special at such a young age.

The Russian winters and constant cold are special occasions—a separate life force with its own personality. It was freezing cold—fierce that night. Everything was frozen around us. It seemed that there was no power capable of reviving sleeping nature. The cold, the cold alone, inexorably permeated the hearts of those ever thirsting for heat and light.

Jumping up while boarding the bus, I squeezed closer to her. She kept thinking about something, but now she was completely different, just like everyone else. Seeing my gaze, she looked away. I decided something.

Leaning over her, I whispered, "Girl, I'm dying!"

She flinched in surprise, and then looked at me in astonishment and suddenly laughed. She continued to laugh, and I frantically thought about my next step. She suddenly stopped laughing and looked at me. Unable to bear her gaze, I lowered my eyes. She went to the exit. But luck accompanied me. Getting out of the bus, she slipped, but having run up behind her, I carefully supported her then I stepped aside with an innocent expression on my face. She looked at me again and smiled. What a smile it was! I guess I would have sacrificed much for that smile. That cold evening, it was as if I was doused with life-giving warmth emanating from the very human heart. I approached her and looked at her beautiful face for a long time. Her chubby, slightly parted lips attracted unknown force.

"So, what happened to you?" she asked, and her lips formed a smile again.

I could not understand what was happening to me. A beautiful girl in front of me was looking at me with big, caressing eyes. I could not say a word; a strange state overwhelmed me, as if I was delirious.

Finally, I muttered, "Now, in the church, when I saw you, your eyes, I realized that I need you like air. It seems to me that I have known you all my life."

Women came and went from my life, leaving no deep traces in it. But then, the fear that she would say "no" took possession of me. I was trembling all over, feeling my powerlessness.

Squinting her eyes, she asked: "You are not cold?"

Just now I noticed that I was standing without a cap and in a splayed coat.

"Here. You have my phone number. Call me tomorrow at 9 o'clock in the evening," she said, and doused me with the warmth of her amazing eyes.

"And now I ask you not to follow me," she said slowly. "I promise that I will see you very soon. But I am afraid that after the meeting—." Without saying it, she turned and went. I watched her for a long time, and suddenly I remembered that I forgot to ask her name.

"What is your name?!" I shouted in a hoarse voice. But she kept going without looking back. I ran after her. Having caught up with her, I looked into her face. I cried out in horror: instead of a beautiful, familiar face, the wrinkled face of an old woman with a grinning, toothless mouth looked at me. I do not know how long I ran. Finally, stumbling, I buried myself in a snowdrift. The cold snow sobered me up.

What's happening? Who is she? These questions did not give me rest. All night, I did not close my eyes. And in the morning, without waiting for the evening, I decided to call my mysterious stranger. After the fourth long beep, she picked up the phone on the other end of the wire. I was silent, not daring to speak.

"I'm listening to you," I heard a familiar voice on the phone say, "speak."

"Hello," I said in a broken voice. "It's me. I was with you yesterday."

"Aw, that's you. How did you get home yesterday?"

I had a thought. Didn't I dream about all this yesterday? She spoke to me as if nothing had happened: in a caressing, caring voice, as before during our first acquaintance. But I remember I reached my home and that the owner of the apartment where I rented a room opened the door for me and looked at me in a frightened way. Going to the mirror, I did not recognize myself: a pale, elongated, anxious face with glittering eyes, a coat in the snow, a scarf dragged at my feet, a hat in my hand. So, it was not a dream.

In the meantime, she waited for an answer.

"I got home well, thanks—thank you," I said. "When can we see you?"

"And you didn't change your mind?" It sounded to me a little like mocking, but at the same time, she asked, with barely noticeable longing in her voice. "Apparently, you are not a bad person, and if anything, I'm sorry," my stranger added quietly.

Her last words sounded so mysterious and with an obvious hint at something that in that instant I wanted to hang up and stop this whole story. But I imagined her smiling, beautiful face and tender eyes and all doubts again dissipated.

In the evening, we met. Olesya—so was the name of my new friend—came almost exactly at the appointed time. The evening was spent in a small cozy cafe, which we visited at the suggestion of Olesya. Here they knew her and were, it seemed to me, very happy. I justified this to myself based on her sociability and simplicity of character. The next evening, Olesya invited me to her apartment. We sat in the kitchen and drank coffee. Olesya told me about her life:

"My father often came home drunk and began to swear and beat my mother. I cried. In the beginning, it stopped my father. He approached me, hugged me, wiped my childhood tears, and promised that this would not happen again. But the next day, everything was repeated: fight, beating, tears. Then my father stopped paying attention to me at all. The scandals at home became more frequent. I was then nine or ten years old. My mother meekly endured all the suffering. There was no one to stand up for us. Of the relatives, there was no one, and the neighbors pretended not to see anything. Nobody wanted to interfere in the affairs of others; all lived closed in their apartments, as if in cages. Even then, I felt a terrible thing—human indifference. I remember how, after another drunken scandal, my father, right in his clothes, fell asleep. A few minutes later, he was snoring loudly. Mother laid me down, sat beside me, and silently looked at me with tears in her eyes. I did not know then that my mother was already seriously ill. Two months later, she died. I stayed with my father. My father began to come home less and less and finally disappeared. Since then, nothing interests me. I've lost trust in people, and the only comfort I find is in God." Then she calmly added, "Our lives and the entire country are going through the most difficult times and it is going to be worse."

The next day, I tried to call her, but nobody picked up the phone. I kept calling the day after and almost every day: no reply. I decided to go to her apartment. I rang the bell; an elderly woman opened the door.

When I asked about Olesya, the woman said that there was no such person and there never had been at that address. I told my friend Elchin about the incident. He suggested I not go there alone; the world was becoming very dangerous. We went there together. Nobody opened the door this time and we left. A few years later, similar to Olesya and her father before that, the entire country disappeared, like it never had existed before. Elchin told me that it was my imagination, a reflection of the emotions and stresses we all were going through. It was likely the case.

In 1989, at age thirty-three, I decided it was time for me to marry. I had been spending many evenings after work walking along residential streets, looking into the apartments of men and women and their families, and suddenly I felt very lonely. I come from a culture where arranged marriages are still customary. I believed that if I could meet a young woman who I liked and liked me, I could convince her family to allow her to marry me.

I did just that. I asked my supervisor at the Red Cross for a week off to return to Baku to find a bride. He looked at me like I was absolutely out of my mind, but he decided to take me up on the challenge and let me go. My family knew of my plan and had lined several dates up for me, but it was too structured. It felt too traditional, too much like the arranged marriages of the past. I wanted a relationship that at least reflected, in some way, the times in which we were living, and I wanted the attraction between my bride and myself to be mutual and independent of our families. During one of my last days home riding bus #65, I saw her. She was at the front of the bus holding onto some books. I moved up to where she was seated and asked her for the time—admittedly not the most creative introductory remark, but it worked. I was able to continue the conversation until she disembarked. By that time, I had learned her name—Leila—and obtained a phone number. Truth is, I was not as successful as I believed myself to be, because she had given me her aunt's phone number and not her own. But I was undeterred. I returned to Moscow without my bride, but I truly hoped and believed it would only be a matter of time. I was persistent. Leila's aunt and I had many telephone conversations over the next few months. She was indeed an excellent gatekeeper. She delayed my meeting with Leila until she was sure I was honest and sincere in my quest.

Finally, a family meeting was arranged. I flew back to Baku and met with Leila and her family at the appointed time. My mother and older brother joined me. Her family was fifteen people strong, including aunts, uncles, and grandparents. I have taken a lot of exams in my life, but I was the most nervous for this one. I took a deep breath and told them everything I thought they would want to know. I told them I was healthy, educated, had a good job, and would take good care of Leila. I told them my worst fault was my single-mindedness when pursuing a goal. They turned from me and conversed among each another, and then smiles broke out on all of their faces. I passed, I won, I got the deal! They approved. They brewed some sweet tea, which traditionally marked the family blessing, and, on December 12, 1989, we were married.

The next day, we left for Moscow. When I was coming to Baku, my close friend Elchin was with me on the same flight. I did not tell him about the real reason for my travel to Baku, because I was not sure of the outcome. His return flight was also the same. When he asked me about the lady with me at the airport, I replied that she was my wife. First, he did not believe me, thinking that I was joking. When he realized that I was telling the truth, he was shocked that I could achieve my goal to get married just by making a couple of brief trips to Baku and meeting my future wife for about twenty minutes on the bus. When we arrived in Moscow, it was a beautiful introduction to the city. A light snow had fallen, and the city was silent and glistening. My new bride had never been away from her family and had never traveled out of Azerbaijan. I believe in omens, and it was a good omen. Neither of us has ever regretted our decision.

During my time there, Moscow suffered from a severe housing shortage. The remedy was communal housing, or *kommunalka*. I had already been living in the kommunalka when I met my wife. It was actually an improvement from my previous living quarters, which included renting space from a temperamental alcoholic who threw me out the door with no forewarning. It was so bad that one night I was forced to sleep in the train station because I had nowhere else to go. The kommunalka is the quintessential Communist incarnation. It is a living unit in which several families share a bathroom and a kitchen. Privacy, such as it is, can only be achieved in the bedroom. It was more like living in a barracks or dormitory than in an apartment. Leila and I shared a three-room flat located near the Medvedkovo metro station that included a communal area and two bedrooms. When I left for Baku the second time in hopes of bringing Leila back as my wife, the woman with whom I shared the apartment, Olga Ivanovna, was quite ill. I never thought she liked me very much during our time together, but I later learned it was merely a reflection of the pain she endured daily. As I was about to leave for the airport, Olga called out to me. For the second time in my life, I entered a room where death hovered overhead. Her son and daughter were at her side. She said goodbye and wished me luck. She died the next day. Leila and I attended the funeral together. Olga's son told me it was his mother's wish that I take her bedroom, which was the bigger of the two. Unfortunately, before we were able to make the exchange, Olga's longtime friend arranged for a man named Evgeniy to take over the space.

Evgeniy was an alcoholic and prone to violent episodes. He was divorced but remained obsessed with his former wife and frequently forced his way into our bedroom, looking for her and accusing me of having sex with her. Despite this, my memories of romancing my new wife in that strange environment leave me with a sweet taste instead of a bitter one. We were unknown to one another, and my wife was barely out of her teens and inexperienced. In the early days of our marriage, she would follow me around the apartment as if playing a child's game and mimic everything I did. Finally, we would break into peals of laughter. We still do whenever we remember our lives there.

Before we celebrated our first anniversary, our daughter was born, and I decided it was time to get away from Evgeniy. Because of my employment, I was able to arrange for my family to move to a single, noncommunal apartment. It was a sixth-floor walk-up, smaller than the kommunalka and on a noisier street, but it was far more private and located near a shaded area where Leila could walk with our daughter in the new perambulator we purchased. The day we were to leave, Evgeniy came into our apartment very drunk and very belligerent. When asked, he refused to leave. Fearing for the safety of my wife and daughter, I pushed him outside. My pent-up anger with that lunatic reached deadly proportions. I forced him down and smashed his face repeatedly into the ground. Finally, I was pulled away by a concerned neighbor who didn't want to see my wife and child abandoned while I served time in jail for murder. My small family moved the next day and stayed in the new apartment until we left Moscow two years later.

On March 11, 1985, Mikhail Gorbachev was elected general secretary of the Communist Party and de facto ruler of the Soviet Union. The world changed. When he came to power, the Soviet economy was failing, worsened by miners' strikes. Store shelves were empty. Some of the Soviet republics continued to call for greater independence, and ethnic conflicts in Transcaucasia (which includes Armenia, Georgia, and Azerbaijan) were accelerating. Gorbachev transformed the Soviet Union. His policies of *glasnost* (openness) and *perestroika* (restructuring) gave the populace a sense of power and a taste of freedom that was the ultimate undoing of a seventy-year union among the republics. For the first time, representatives of foreign countries came to the Soviet Union to invest and exchange goods and ideas.

The entire structure of Soviet society as I had known it began to shift. At the time, I was unsure how I felt about it. Fortunes were being made, but it seemed as though the people who were making them were the same people who had been in power during the old system. Independent newspapers, magazines, television, and radio popped up. The *Ploshad Nogina* (the square named after Nogin in Russian) where I worked was situated across from a quiet park. Before Gorbachev's reforms, an elderly woman used to sweep the square every morning. Every morning I would say hello to her, and she would reply, "Good morning, son."

Then the character of the Ploshad Nogina changed; it became a gathering place for new Russian businessmen, complete with cell phones, laptop computers, and prostitutes. Clothing styles changed. Even the manner of talking to other people changed. Life became louder and more frenetic. Restaurants popped up along the plaza like mushrooms. One afternoon, I decided to try one. The obsequious waiter fawned all over me, insisting on seating me near a window that was unobstructed so that I could watch the activities outside, unfolding my napkin and pouring me a glass of water with just the correct number of ice cubes. Then he brought the menu. The prices were, to my mind, outrageous and unreachable, and I left. So, apparently, did the elderly woman. It was not a course of steady progress forward. Perestroika in theory should have led to greater debate and understanding among the different populations of the Soviet Union; instead, it created an opportunity for many to express long-held ethnic hatred with little fear of reprisal. People like myself were jeered at on the street, and one time, my wife was threatened while waiting in line to purchase food.

It's all in the language, in the definitions, in the types of words you use: comrade instead of friend, microrayon instead of home or apartment, Azeri or Armenian or Georgian instead of citizen. The heat and fire from the mixing of races and ethnicities in the United States created a melting pot. In the Soviet Union, those same elements only served to create greater friction and separation among its people.

During the period of perestroika, things turned ugly and unpredictable. The children of Communism had never been taught how to deal with freedom, and the state as parent had been too restrictive during their youth. The release of state control over all things created a vacuum. The population acted as though a bunch of ill-behaved teenagers who no longer needed to heed common rules of civility. The disintegration and ultimate demise of Communism as a system was a good thing, but its unexpected and unintended consequences have led to a proliferation of ethnic conflicts—first among the people of the former Soviet republics and later in the Middle East, which was no longer controlled through the balance of power between the Soviet Union and the United States.

The changes initiated by perestroika and glasnost were beginning to have an effect on my career. In November 1990, I left the Red Cross and began employment at the League of Scientific and Industrial Associations of the USSR. As chief expert interpreter of the International Department, I was part of a team responsible for developing economic and trade relations between the Soviet Union, the United States, Canada, and Japan. It was one of the first organizations created specifically for the purpose of opening up Soviet markets to foreign investors, and it was my first opportunity to work with educators and businessmen from the West. The president of the association was a former influential employee of the Central Committee, Arcady Volsci, who wisely used his contacts within the Communist system to secure his position in the association. It turned out to be a very successful move for him. Others who failed to adapt quickly found themselves in unfamiliar positions of ordinariness. They soon lost all the accoutrements of privilege—some with very dire results. Dmitry Lisovolik, who I reported to at the International Department of the Central Committee of the Communist Party, was one such individual. No longer invited to shop at the stores reserved for the party elite, he was required to stand in line with the rest of the masses to purchase food. He was unable to tolerate his change in circumstance. Rumors circulated that his wife had a bad character, which contributed to his ultimate decision to commit suicide on a day he had failed to purchase food and returned home empty-handed.

My boss at work asked me to assist the family of Dmitry Lisovolik with funeral arrangements, because I knew him personally. Therefore, I spent some time with his wife and newly arrived son from overseas, where he was studying, to make the necessary arrangements.

It was a frightening omen of events to come. Western journalists showed up at Lisovolik's funeral. They were quietly convinced to leave, having been given the party line that all was well with Soviet society. My boss showed me a few men who were keeping low profiles at the funeral and explained to me that they were from the GRU, *Glavnoye Razvedyvatel-*

noye Upravleniye (main intelligence directorate). There was little discussion about the change in the political and economic climate at my place of employment, at least with me. I was outside the loop of the powerful and connected. Those with whom I did converse seemed, like me, cautious. We had grown up believing in the Communist system, and it was hard to accept that changes were permanent. We were convinced that despite the rhetoric, the KGB (the notorious Soviet intelligence agency) continued to have eyes and ears everywhere, and it was only a matter of time until things would return to normal and those who were too vocal would be jailed or worse.

A month after I joined the team at the League of Scientific and Industrial Associations of the USSR, I was hired by Luna-Trading Inc. to help coordinate economic and trade activities between Japan and the USSR. In addition, I was working on my PhD, hoping that the new era of glasnost would allow me the opportunity to travel. Still, prospects continued to pass me by. Control seemed to shift from the Kremlin to individual mafioso, who were even more brutal in their grab for power. In spite of many promises, I was never asked to join any of my employers on their trips overseas. In truth, the policies of perestroika and glasnost, which were meant to open Soviet society, were impediments to my opportunities for advancement. And I was not alone. Government, Soviet culture, and the economy were crumbling. In an effort to save the system, Gorbachev negotiated a new union treaty that would have converted the Soviet Union into a federation of independent republics. On August 19, 1991, the day before the treaty was to be signed, a group of hardline Communists attempted a coup d'état. The putsch of August 19 through 22 was a dizzying three days.

I awoke on the 19th to news reports that Gorbachev had suddenly taken ill and power was being transferred to vice president Gennady Yanayev and the newly formed State Committee for a State of Emergency, or GK-ChP. A chill ran down my spine upon learning that the committee was composed of the leaders of the KGB, the military, and the police. I was not frightened, but I am cautious by nature, and I arrived at work careful not to respond to the comments and questions of my colleagues. Nothing seemed out of the ordinary, except perhaps there appeared to be more police on the street than was typical. Later that morning, I heard a low rumble and the floor shook. The central boulevards in Moscow are unusually broad, designed for military control. Within hours, most of them were filled with tanks and armored personnel carriers. I tried to maintain my routine during those three days, but entering and leaving the building sometimes proved difficult. On the first day of the putsch, hundreds of people filled the Ploschad Nogina, and some of the demonstrators tried to break into our building. Arkady Volsci, the president of Scientific and Industrial Associations, managed to convince the crowd that our organization had nothing to do with the Central Committee of the Communist Party, even though we shared space with them on the Ploschad Nogina.

Later that day, troops surrounded the area and kept the crowds at bay during the remainder of the uprising. I kept my distance, as I did not want to anger any of the weapon-toting soldiers. I could still remember the steel-toed kick to my ribs. I also did not want to participate in demonstrations. I am a quiet man, and as an interpreter, I am by nature an observer; more importantly, I had a young wife and child, and I was responsible for their safety. Each day, more people filled the streets. Many approached the tanks; some stood in their path while others stuck flowers in the guns. At one point, I watched a mob of people storm Dzerzhinsky Square, the place where the KGB was headquartered. Felix Edmundovich Dzerzhinsky was widely recognized as the father of the notorious intelligence agency, a ruthless murderer who was responsible for the death of millions in the early years of the Russian revolution. A number of people tried in vain to topple the statute of Dzerzhinsky. What was odd was that the KGB brutes just stood on the roof of their building, quietly watching. There was an unreal quality to the whole affair, almost as if it were completely orchestrated on both the part of the military and the crowds. In fact, I was unable to shake that feeling during the entire event, and I was unwilling to become a tool used by others for their own gain.

Later, I went back to Dzerzhinsky Square, curious to see what was going on there. A crowd was still milling about, and there was a frightening energy in the air. The doors to the KGB and Central Committee of the Communist Party buildings had the word "fascists" spray-painted across them, and several of the doors and windows to the buildings had been smashed. The Dzerzhinsky statute lay prone on the ground. I asked a man standing near me what had happened, and he explained to me that a crane had come and brought the statue down, all under the noses of the KGB! Again, I couldn't shake the feeling that this was someone's dangerous game of chess. I saw no future in it, and I instinctively knew I would soon be starting over.

By August 20, all independent news agencies were officially shut down. A couple of them resorted to handing out flyers to keep everyone abreast of developments. Curfews were imposed, and mass gatherings were banned. Younger people still openly discussed events in public places, but older people were much more cautious, still uncertain how events would play out. At home, I turned on the television to see if I could learn more about what was happening. Central Television was broadcasting the ballet *Swan Lake* of all things.

Police began checking passports and identification papers. And more than once I saw Russian officers abusing non-Russians. It was open season. I approached one such policeman and asked him why he was mistreating a young man. He responded to me by saying all Caucasians were criminals and should be treated as such. I was speechless. I felt I was safe, because I had a *propiska*, a document that proved I was a proper resident of Moscow, which was particularly difficult for nonprofessional Caucasians to obtain, but under those conditions, I was afraid the situation could change at any moment.

Then, on August 22 it was all over. Gorbachev was miraculously healed but severely weakened politically. It was time for me to go home.

Interlude

Demise of the Empire

Lessons Learned from British, Soviet, and US Campaigns in Afghanistan and Iraq

The US strategy advocates a military strike and increased civil development while making the protection of civilians a higher priority, an endeavor to attain more popular support in order to not repeat the mistakes of the unsuccessful Soviet experience in Afghanistan.[1]

During the military operations in and among indigenous cultures, the protection of civilians should remain a higher priority. This author has had firsthand observations of the importance of human factors throughout his life experiences over the decades. These experiences included his service in the Soviet army in the 1970s, as a senior diplomat during global geopolitical changes in the early 1990s, and in related bloody conflicts such as the Nagorno-Karabakh conflict, which erupted across the post–Soviet, post–Warsaw Pact space; his observations in Iraq while deployed with the US Army in 2004–2005; and his trip to Ukraine as part of the US Army study in 2016, among many other experiences. These still-unresolved ethnic, territorial, and religious conflicts, which the author witnessed in Iraq, Russia, Azerbaijan, Ukraine, and elsewhere, are disturbingly similar in nature. They have been always manipulated by different political agendas, and they have always led to tragedies and the suffering of ordinary people.

Despite painful British, Soviet, and other experiences in Afghanistan and elsewhere, it is not surprising for this author—who was the first US Army culture and foreign language advisor, hired as a result of US campaigns in Afghanistan and Iraq—that it had taken the United States time to create and refine its cultural and language training, which is becoming again a lesser priority with a new large-scale combat operations (LSCO) concept. Although a Russian proverb says, "You do not learn from others' mistakes but you only really learn from your own mistakes," the history and present times show that we never learn and continue making the same mistakes over and over again.

This chapter is examining insight factors that might be important for military strategists, policy makers, and academics or general audiences alike who are seeking to understand Taliban propaganda; its influence strategy; the differences and similarities among the Afghan, Iraqi, and other insurgencies; and their historical and sociocultural factors. Analysis is based on Western and regional sources but primarily on the experiences and observations of the author. The United States never completely understood the nature of other cultures—or the causes and origins of their regional conflicts. Part of the reason could be its history and geography, simply being across the ocean from European and Eurasian regions that were the main theaters of two devastating global conflicts and that are currently undergoing another major geopolitical transformation since the end of World War II and the Cold War era. Nevertheless, in a survey of Afghan cities, a report released by the Pentagon in April 2010 classified twenty-one Afghan cities as being in support of the government while forty-eight other cities were cited as inclining to back the Taliban forces.[2] The report also highlighted the current state of the insurgency, including its strengths and weaknesses. It's *strengths* are below:

- The speed and decisiveness of insurgent information operations (IO) and media campaigns remain not only the insurgents' main effort but also their most significant strength.
- Organizational capabilities and operational reach are qualitatively and geographically expanding.
- The ability to intimidate through targeted killings and threats in order to force acquiescence to their will is growing.
- The strength and ability of shadow governance to discredit the authority and legitimacy of the Afghan government is increasing.

Improvised explosive device (IED) use is increasing in numbers and complexity. IEDs are as much a tactic and process as they are a weapon. Insurgents' tactics, techniques, and procedures for conducting complex attacks are increasing in sophistication and strategic effect.

According to the report, insurgent *weaknesses and vulnerabilities* are as follows:[3]

- The insurgency includes multiple locally based tribal networks as well as layered command structures, which at times can make coordinated execution difficult.
- Persistent fissures among insurgent leadership persist at local levels.
- The insurgency is dependent on many marginalized/threatened segments of the Pashto population.
- The insurgency is over reliant on external support.

Insurgent violence against civilians and respected figures can be counterproductive.

The Soviet experiment about forty years ago showed that in spite of the Soviets' powerful military establishment, they were losing the war even though they were winning the battle to some degree. The main reason was that they did not manage to "win [the] hearts and minds"[4] of the local populace, although they made extensive use of Soviet Tajiks, Uzbeks, and similar ethnic people who were similar in cultural heritage to Afghanistan's in special and other operations in an attempt to acquire favoritism of the populace. Yet, these Soviets were predominantly associated with ethnic Russian "infidels" (literally "unfaithful").[5]

According to former Spetsnaz (*otrayadi spetsialnogo naznacheniya* in Russian, literally meaning "special purpose forces") and other Soviet military service members, when insurgents ambushed and captured ethnic Russian troops, they would behead them. When Soviets of Tajik, Uzbek, Kirgiz, or other Central Asian origin were captured, the insurgents would sometimes give them copies of the Holy Book and let them go if they acknowledged their allegiance to Islam and the Koran. The degree of alienation toward Soviets was very significant. They could never overcome this alienation despite their active counterinsurgency operations (COIN) activities, mainly conducted by culturally and linguistically trained KGB and elite Special Forces units operating inside

Afghanistan. The Pentagon report acknowledged that the United States has problems in the same area but is making efforts to overcome them.

The Resemblance of Mujahedeen and Taliban "Hearts and Minds" Campaigns[6]

This was the Taliban leader Mullah Omar's COIN guidance at the time, a population-centric strategy that was geared toward "winning [the] hearts and minds" of the local population and maintaining their loyalty. It says:

- Keep people and their property safe. Do not let those who love money take our local people's property and cause them problems.
- Keep good relations with your friends and the local people, and do not let the enemy divide/separate you.

Taliban leadership also clearly defined its tactics toward coalition forces:

- We do not have to beat the International Security Assistance Force (ISAF) militarily; outlast international will to remain in Afghanistan.
- Continue population outreach and protection programs.
- Continue successful asymmetric operations.
- Expand lethal IED and high-profile attacks to deny ISAF freedom of movement.
- Make the main enemy the United States.

Afghan Taliban directives also include prohibitions on:

- Mistreating the population
- Forcibly taking personal weapons
- Taking children to conduct jihad
- Forcing people to pay donations
- Searching homes
- Kidnapping people for money

This book was given to each Taliban fighter as guidance. It has thirteen chapters and sixty-seven articles and lays out what one can and cannot do. The following are some key quotes that outline the new code of conduct:

> **On asylum**: Every Muslim can invite anyone working for the slave government in Kabul to leave their job and cut their relationship with this corrupt administration. If the person accepts, then with the permission of the provincial and district leadership, a guarantee of safety can be given.[7]
>
> **On prisoners**: Whenever any official, soldier, contractor, or worker of the slave government is captured, these prisoners cannot be attacked or harmed.[8]
>
> The decision on whether to seek a prisoner exchange, or to release the prisoner, with a strong guarantee, will be made by the provincial leader. Releasing prisoners in exchange for money is strictly prohibited.
>
> If the prisoner is a director, a commander, or a district chief or higher, the decision on whether to harm, kill, release, or forgive them is only made by the Imam or deputy Imam.
>
> If a military infidel is captured, the decision on whether to kill, release, or exchange the hostage is only to be made by the Imam or deputy Imam.
>
> **On civilian casualties**: Governors, district chiefs, and line commanders and every member of the Mujahedeen must do their best to avoid civilian deaths, civilian injuries, and damage to civilian property. Great care must be taken.[9]
>
> **On suicide attacks**: Suicide attacks should only be used on high and important targets. A brave son of Islam should not be used for lower and useless targets. The utmost effort should be made to avoid civilian casualties.[10]
>
> **On unity**: Creating a new Mujahedeen group or battalion is forbidden. If unofficial groups or irregular battalions refuse to join the formal structure, they should be disbanded. If a governor or leader has in the past had a unit or active group in another province, they should bring it to the attention of the leader of that province. That leader should then take over command of the group.
>
> **On relations with the Afghan people**: The Mujahedeen have to behave well and show proper treatment to the nation, in order to

bring the hearts of civilian Muslims closer to them. The Mujahedeen must avoid discrimination based on tribal roots, language, or their geographic background.[11]

Below is an English translation of some quotes from the speeches of Mullah Mohammed Omar, an Afghan mujahadeen commander who led the Taliban and founded the Islamic Emirate of Afghanistan in 1996. These quotes are also part of the bylaws:[12]

Dear Mujahedeen Brothers:

All your intentions and deeds should be according to God's edicts and the Prophet's guidelines. Stand like steel when confronting the enemy. Incidents [failures] and propaganda should not shake your will. Be sincere to your friends [fellow fighters] and civilian populace; sustain the strong bonds of loyalty and brotherhood, so that the enemy must not succeed in achieving his evil goals of splitting our ranks. In your work and operations take good precautions and consultations and use wisdom and intelligence. Do not let your personal beliefs, emotions, haste, and carelessness interfere [in your judgment], when punishing someone. Protecting people's lives and property is a major goal of Jihad. Governors should not harass people for their own personal and material gains.

The people of Laghman Province were addressed this night letter (threat letter):[13]

Islamic Emirate of Afghanistan Announcement

Greetings to the Muslim and Mujahedeen residents of Laghman Province

Respected Friends,

God has said "oh Muslims, do not associate and become friends with Jews and Christians [Americans, British, and other 'infidels'], because their friends are those who support them [as we see them]. And whoever became friend with them will therefore be considered one of them. And their end result and death will be like them [Jews and Christians]." So we announce that:

Those people who live in Laghman Province and work with them (Americans, British, and others), should stop working there and cooperate with Taliban and Mujahedeen. Otherwise, they should leave Laghman and go and live with their American overlords. If not, they do not have the right to complain later (they will take the consequences).

It is being announced to all those people who cooperate with the infidels, aggressors, and traitors, to stop their shameful acts and instead work for and support their beloved country and preach on behalf of the true children of the land. They are responsible for the dire consequences if they do not obey these commands.

It should be said to the informants that they have been exposed and they do not have any place to run and hide. And we warn them not to side with the Americans in persecuting and martyring ordinary civilians, children, elders, and women. Otherwise, God willing, they will not be able to run from the Mujahedeen.

Muslims in general, (religious) scholars, Mullahs, and Imams should understand that according to the above quote from the Quran, they cannot perform at the funeral ceremony of an informant and traitor because such people belong to them (infidels). So our Muslim brothers should understand this issue (in a religious sense) and should not participate in the funerals of people who are traitors of their nation and faith. (Religious) Scholars, Mullahs, and Imams should seriously consider their own safety as the results may not be pleasant.

It is the duty of Mullahs and Imams to announce this message to their followers.

These examples indicate major efforts by Taliban leadership to "win [the] hearts and minds" of the people while endeavoring to intimidate the local populace and prevent it from cooperating with the Afghan government and coalition forces. Coalition forces were facing tremendous security and information operations (IO) challenges from a sophisticated and adaptive enemy that was well versed in local psychology, culture, and traditions.

But the insurgency in Afghanistan was not monolithic and unified. Many leaders of different groups were allied with the Taliban and al-Qaeda at the time, the main reason being that their tactical and strategic interests coincided. They were supported by the same elements of Pakistan's

Inter-Services Intelligence Directorate (ISID) and other Pakistani and regional forces that also supported Afghan and other regional and global holy Muslim worriers who came to Afghanistan to fight against the Soviet invasion. In 1989, the Soviet army withdrew from Afghanistan. But this time, support was mainly focused on a strategic counterbalance to India and other countries. Compared to the Soviet invasion of Afghanistan, however, when mujahadeen (or those engaged in jihad) were supported by at least two major powers such as the United States and China, the current Afghan insurgency did not seem to enjoy the kind of consistent state-level support from major powers such as China or Russia.

There were some unconfirmed reports of the Shia Islamic Republic of Iran supporting a Sunni Taliban insurgency. But if the foreign forces withdrew, it was believed that different insurgency groups would turn their guns against each other, vying for power as happened after the Soviet withdrawal from Afghanistan in 1989. The confusion regarding which "strategic side" the US-led coalition forces were on also fueled the Afghan and Iraqi insurgencies. The removal of Saddam Hussein's government in Iraq created a vacuum in the regional strategic counterbalance toward its archenemy, the Shia Islamic Republic of Iran.

Iraq and Afghanistan Insurgencies Compared

Al-Qaeda (from the Arabic meaning "base") is an organization with global aims. It could operate, if the opportunity arose, in any corner of the world. It is seen as a decentralized franchise network with multiple branches mainly active in the Middle East, Central and South Asia, and Africa. Their original leaders, the late Osama bin Laden and his deputy Ayman al-Zawahiri, were believed to be closer in their ideology to the concept of the conflict of civilizations, actively using the "Islamic factor" as the banner for mobilizing new recruits.[14]

However, their weakness was clearly reflected in Iraq when they declared *Umma* (in Arabic with religious content, meaning "Islamic brotherhood"), mostly of foreign fighters belonging to Al-Qaeda, and did not get their desired support within the local population. The factor of alienation also played a role when around one hundred thousand former Iraqi insurgents, formerly allied with al-Qaeda, turned against them. Why did it happen? Three factors contributed to this result.

First, although former insurgents in the predominantly western Iraqi province of Anbar are Sunni Muslims and similar to the members of al-Qaeda, the majority of homegrown Iraqi insurgents were not attracted by the Islamic political slogans of al-Qaeda. They were mostly former Ba'ath Party members with an ideology based on Pan-Arab nationalism rather than Islamism.[15] Saddam Hussein himself was considered a secular politician who was trying to explore the Islamic factor at some points for political reasons, but his Pan-Arab nationalistic ideology was secular in nature.

Second, compared to Afghanistan, the more educated and urbanized population of Iraq had already enjoyed close political, military, economic, and cultural ties with the West in the past. These factors made Iraq more prepared for cooperation with Western governments and coalition forces. The growth of other insurgency groups in Iraq and the growing influence of Iran made the future of Iraq very uncertain.

Third, the terrain and difference in histories between Afghanistan and Iraq created conflict. Afghanistan mostly consists of rugged mountains with plains in the north and southwest. It's landlocked. Geography and history played a significant role in the sociopolitical, economic, and cultural formation of the country. It also affected the Afghan psyche and its social differentiation. Today, one can say that Afghanistan is mostly at the medieval socioeconomic level of development with very diversified tribal and ethnic societal systems.

The above factors significantly explain why many experts and policy makers expect that the task of stabilizing Afghanistan presents more challenges than in Iraq.

Past and Present Insurgent Leaders in Afghanistan

Along with the Taliban, the majority of the insurgency groups in Afghanistan are homegrown, united under the same Islamic banner and against the predominantly Western coalition forces. This is their strength, because it is very easy to justify their actions against the "foreign invading factor." Their knowledge of the local indigenous cultures and psychologies are additional advantages for the very diverse insurgency network. Among them are:

Warlord Gulbuddin Hekmatyar studied engineering at Kabul University in the 1970s. He established the Hizb-i-Islami (Islamic Party) to counter growing Soviet influence and occupation in the 1980s. He is allied to the Taliban. Hekmatyar's goal is the independent Islamic State and restoring Afghan sovereignty. Fighters have a reputation for being more educated than the Taliban: "Hizb-i-Islami will fight our jihad until foreign troops are gone from Afghanistan and Afghans have set up an Islamic Government."[16]

Jalaluddin Haqqani is an anti-Soviet war veteran and an early advocate of the "Afghan Arabs" joining the jihad against the Soviet Union. Elements of the Haqqani network work closely with al-Qaeda. Reportedly, he was based in Waziristan and supported by Pakistan's ISID but died some time ago. Presently, day-to-day operations of the network are conducted by his son Sirajuddin or Siraj Haqqani.

In 2007, Baitullah Mehsud (reportedly killed by US air strike) had formed Pakistani Taliban groups into a single organization. He was replaced by Hakimullah Mehsud (from the same Mehsud tribe). The Mehsud tribe, mostly located in the rough, isolated geographic center of South Waziristan, has a long history of militant and insurgent activities against non-Pashtun and governmental political control. The group, also referred to as the "Pakistani Taliban," have strong links to al-Qaeda. The reason for the organization's Pakistani focus is the perception that the Pakistani government betrayed Pakistani national interests by collaborating with the West and coalition forces.

Strategically, their goal in the fight is against the West and its ideological concepts. But one should remember that the Taliban as the movement was created by Pakistani politicians at the time of former prime minister Benazir Bhutto, who was allied with the West. It was created as a strategic tool and counterbalance that was vying for influence in the region, mainly against India. Ironically, the Pakistani Taliban was believed to be behind the assassination of Bhutto, the main architect of the movement. Former ISID chief general Hamid Gul was directly involved in the creation and support of the Taliban and other Islamist groups, according to Ahmed Rashid, the author of *Taliban: Militant Islam, Oil and Fundamentalism in Central Asia*.[17] Gul believed that if the West had to negotiate with Afghan insurgents, then they had to deal only with the late Mullah Omar, because he was the only principal leader of the Taliban in Afghanistan. But one can argue against this for two reasons. First, although Mullah Omar was still the primary spiritual leader, he was not the primary political day-to-day operations leader of the insurgency. Second, he was the creation and a tool of mostly Pakistani intelligence services and likely continued to exist due to their support until 2013.

But for many ordinary Afghans, especially of the Pashto tribes of the east and south, as well as for Taliban fighters and other homegrown insurgents of Afghanistan, the symbolic charismatic image of Mullah Omar fits perfectly in the Afghan ethnocultural psychology in the same way the charismatic "Mad Mullah," Fakir of Ipi (Mirza Ali Khan) did, who battled the British during the first Anglo-Afghan war of 1839 to 1842.[18] This period marked the "great game," a power struggle between Russia and Britain for dominance in the region. Britain occupied Afghanistan and used it as a buffer to protect British India from Russian influence. Ultimately, this power struggle resulted in the 1893 Durand Line Agreement between the government of colonial British India (now Pakistan) signed by Henry Mortimer Durand and Emir of Afghanistan Amir Abdur Rahman Khan.

The agreement meant to delineate a physical line between their respective spheres of influence. About 1,610 miles long, this line continues to be an area of tension between Afghanistan and Pakistan, but very few across both borders, especially among Pashto tribes, recognize it. The Afghan Taliban is presently intensifying its IO among the locals based on its knowledge of the local customs and culture and nuances of the local psyche. The outcome of the coalition forces' efforts will depend on their ability to gain the trust of ordinary Afghans. It will require specific knowledge and abilities to prepare soldiers for living and working in a new country, preventing culture shock, easing transitions, and creating awareness of different cultural and individual styles to maximize operations. Operating in indigenous cultures rather than in a bipolar strategic environment of the Cold War era (traditional war fighting) adds new dimension to the military's missions in Afghanistan, Iraq, and elsewhere. Operating in joint interagency, intergovernmental, and multinational (JIIM) environments requires a new, more sophisticated set of knowledge and skills that are very different.

The Pashto Influence

As was the case during anti-British and then anti-Soviet Jihad, the insurgency in Afghanistan is composed of Pashto tribes. Between the two main Pashto tribal confederations, Durrani and Ghilzai, the homegrown insurgency mostly consists of Ghilzai tribes. There has been animosity between the two throughout the history of the country. The Durranis, which are mostly in power, include the late Zahir Shah, the last king of Afghanistan, and former president Hamid Karzai. Mullah Omar, who was born in 1961 in Kandahar and is the former spiritual leader of the Taliban movement until 2013, was a Ghilzai of the Hotak tribe.

That is why the maxim "know your enemy"–coined by the famous general, military strategist, writer, and philosopher Sun Tzu–is very important in the current fight in Afghanistan. Understanding cultural factors such as *Pashtunwali* (the way of the Pashto) is very important in understanding and succeeding in Pashto-dominated Afghan society.

What is Pashtunwali? It's an unwritten or informal set of religious, ethnic, tribal, and moral norms that were formed over centuries among the Pashto tribes. This way of life, to a greater extent, is preserved among the so-called hill Pashtuns or highlanders who live in the mountains and are naturally isolated and historically more independent than the so-called lowlanders. These are Pashtuns who live on the cultivated and irrigated plains and tend to be more integrated into Afghan governance and society as a whole and are more subjected to external influences.

The main elements of Pashtunwali include:[19]

- Badal: Right of blood feuds or revenge
- Nunawati: Right of a fugitive to seek refuge and acceptance of his bona-fide offer of peace
- Melmastya: Hospitality and protection to every guest
- Isteqamat: Persistence
- Ghayrat: Defense of property and honor
- Namus: Defense of one's female relatives.

Another feature of Afghan, and specifically Pashto, character: Do not show your emotions, impatience, anger, etc., because it's considered a sign of weakness. Personal relationships, trust, and, most importantly, deeds are crucial elements of winning the hearts and minds of the Afghan people. Knowledge of the local culture and customs would be the ultimate factors in persuading the local populace.

Islam in Afghanistan

Afghans predominantly follow the Sunni Hanafi school of Islam. The Taliban movement belongs to the Hanafi school, with a strict interpretation of Islam known as *Deobandi*, which does not recognize any innovation or modification within Islam since the time of Prophet Mohamed, including Shi'ism, which emerged later. That explains, to a certain extent, the tense relationships between the Shiʿite-dominated Islamic Republic of Iran and the Sunni Taliban government that existed during the second part of the 1990s until the beginning of the 2000s.

My contacts with Afghan expatriates over the years mostly included those who were originally from the Pashto areas of northwest Afghanistan and Nuristan. As always, I enjoyed their firsthand experiences and assessments of different Afghan sociocultural and political situations. One of them told me the story about al-Qaeda members, mostly of Arab origin, who moved to the southern province of Kandahar, the spiritual home of the Taliban, and settled there. In the early 2000s, during the US bombings of the area, many of them were killed. The locals buried them and, over the years, residents have been visiting the burial sites, regarding them as sacred. The perception among the locals was that that the foreign Muslim mujahedeen came to Afghanistan and died for the Afghan cause of fighting the "infidels." Also, according to the expatriates, Taliban and al-Qaeda are not really formalized organizations anymore, by traditional definitions, but rather ideologies with a wider range of influence across geographical boundaries. These ideologies continue to globally attract those who oppose Western culture and its way of life for different reasons. Al-Qaeda is a global terror network and the Taliban is homegrown—mostly an Afghan/Pakistan Pashto tribal-based movement. It seems that it is easier to justify the fight against al-Qaeda than against the Taliban, because the Taliban and its affiliated groups say that they fight against the foreign invasion that is trying to restore Afghanistan's sovereignty.

The "Taliban factor" as viewed in Arab media widely covers the sociocultural, political, and strategic aspects of the Taliban phenomenon that has become a source of encouragement for many Islamic and jihadist organizations around the world. The outcome of the fight is of special importance for the future strategic balances, not only in the region but globally as well.

Psychological features of the movement include obstinacy and the ability to stand up to and face very tough circumstances and hardships. These are applicable to the Afghan people in general and the people of Kandahar in particular, which is in the southern province of the country where the movement was born. There is a very popular game in Kandahar where two competitors place burning coals in their hands. The winner is the one who is able to continue holding the coal until it burns out.

Internal and external factors that led to the prominence of Taliban include the civil wars, the chaos that took place after the defeat of the Soviet Union, corruption, lack of security, and the rapidly attained wealth of warlords.

The external factors are that, first, Pakistan was seeking to exert and maintain influence of the government of Afghanistan to facilitate economic and trade relations with central Asian republics because the post-Soviet Mujahedeen government of Rabbani and Masoud was not actively cooperating with Pakistan, from Pakistan's perspective, enough. That was one of the primary reasons why Pakistan unsuccessfully gave aid to Gulbuddin Hekmetyar, his Hizb-i-Islami group, and Afghan Uzbek leader general Dustam. When the Taliban movement became prominent, Pakistan lost the opportunity to support it.

Second, in the beginning, the United States selectively fought some radical Afghan warlords while at the same time relied on those groups that would be easier to control and influence. Another goal has been to prevent the spread of Iranian influence in the central Asian republics that have the second-biggest oil reserves in the world after the Arab gulf.

According to Arab media, the movement had several goals, which have since gradually undergone changes and adjustments. They were declared by the movement's spokesman Mullah Abdul Mann an Niyazi on November 3, 1994, after capturing the town of Spin Buldak. The main goal then was to restore security, collect weapons from other groups, and eliminate checkpoints that extorted people.

After the spread of Taliban control to other Afghan provinces, the movement declared its new goals. On April 4, 1996, Mullah Muhammad Omar declared that the movement's goals were:[20]

- The establishment of an Islamic government that follows the examples and teachings of the four rightly guided caliphs, or rulers of the Islamic Caliphate.
- That Islam would become the religion of both the people and the government.
- To base the constitution on Islamic Shari'a.
- To choose Muslim scholars for important government positions.
- To destroy the roots of fanaticism and tribal nationalism.
- To protect the people of the Book (Jews, Christians, and Muslims) and their properties, reserving their rights that are given by Islamic Shari'a.
- To improve political ties with all the Islamic countries and organizations according to the rules of Shari'a.
- To require that women wear hijab (headscarfs) in all sectors of Muslim society.
- To fight crime as defined by the Taliban, which included using drugs and viewing forbidden pictures and films.
- To introduce the independent Islamic courts, which should oversee government institutions.
- To establish a trained army to protect the Islamic State against external aggression.
- To base political and international activities on the Quran and Sunna.
- To develop the state economy based on Islamic principles.
- To appeal to Islamic countries to help rebuild Afghanistan.
- To collect Zakat (Islamic taxes) and spend it on appropriate projects and public services.

Pipeline Politics and Its Regional Implications for Afghanistan

The strategic pipeline, called Baku-Tbilisi-Ceyhan (BTC), was inaugurated in 2005. It was the first major pipeline bypassing Russian territory, beginning in Baku, the capital of Azerbaijan, and transiting through the territory of the former Soviet Republic of Georgia toward the Turkish Mediterranean port of Ceyhan. From there, oil is taken by tankers to world markets. Having up to one million barrels per-day capacity, the pipeline has an even more important strategic implication: it will strengthen the political and economic independence of the countries of the region against possible Russian resurgence. But even before completion, it had also marked the beginning of the new "great game" with global and regional powers such as the United States, China, and Russia all vying for influence in the area. Once again, the region became very attractive for global geopolitics, enhanced by the discovery of natural resources in Afghanistan such as natural gas, oil, marble, gold, copper, and chromates.

Because of Afghanistan's important geostrategic location, there were serious plans for oil and natural-gas export pipelines in the second part of 1990s. However, since 1996, the security of most of Afghanistan has been unstable and controlled by the Taliban movement, which the United States did not officially recognize.

Former ambassador John J. Maresca, who was later vice president for international relations of the Unocal Oil Corporation (USA) in the 1990s, in his testimony to the House Subcommittee on Asia and the Pacific on February 12, 1998, concluded his congressional testimony with the following statement: "Developing cost-effective, profitable and efficient export routes for Central Asia resources is a formidable, but not impossible, task. It has been accomplished before. A commercial corridor, a 'new Silk Road,' can link the Central Asia supply with the demand—once again making Central Asia the crossroads between Europe and Asia."[21]

Other Challenges

Among other major challenges within Afghanistan are corruption, criminal activity, and a huge illicit opium trade. The extent of heroin flow from this relatively small country is a regional and global challenge. There are two main problems: First, the Afghan economy is heavily reliant on opium cultivation, which does not allow other sectors of the economy to normally develop, and second, it feeds the insurgency and contributes to the instability of the country and region.[22]

4

A Socialist Democracy

I left for Azerbaijan in the hopes I could take advantage of new opportunities that were arising there. It was clear to me that it was only a matter of time before Azerbaijan claimed independence from the Soviet Union. Whether the Soviet Union would quietly accept that declaration or once again invade my country was unclear. My instincts proved correct: four months later, the Soviet Union ceased to exist.

Soviet leadership sent troops and tanks as a last attempt to prevent the demise of the empire. Azerbaijanis call it "Black January," which is the day when Soviet tanks and troops brutally murdered the civilians in the capital of Azerbaijan, Baku, on January 19 and 20, 1990, to suppress the independence movement. But it was too late, and it only accelerated the collapse of the USSR.

As of December 1991, all of the republics had declared independence. Ethnic conflicts intensified. I have often compared the ethnic conflicts in Iraq to those that exploded after the disintegration of the Soviet Union and wondered how much they really differ from one another. The names changed but the stories are essentially the same.

Given my background in international relations, it seemed my best opportunities lay in the diplomatic corps. Fortunately, when I went back to Baku to explore future prospects, I was able to get an audience with the foreign minister. We had a long, fruitful conversation, and he promised me that if I returned to Baku, he would offer me a job in the ministry. He presented me with a letter of invitation to that effect, and I took him at his word. It was a gamble I almost lost. My colleagues at the International Department of the League of Scientific and Industrial Associations of the USSR were certain that the center of central Asian and South Caucasus power would return and remain in Moscow. They were concerned that the conflict that had recently erupted again in the Nagorno-Karabakh region would overflow into other parts of Azerbaijan, throwing the country into civil war and causing my new diplomatic prospects to evaporate.

The conflict between the Armenians and the Azeris had reignited in 1988. Shusha, my childhood summer playground, was at the center of the conflict. In May 1992, the Armenians launched an offensive and captured Shusha. It was then that my extended family was forced to leave as the city was looted and burned by invading forces. Hedging my bet, I thanked my colleagues who assured me I would always be welcomed back, and I returned to Azerbaijan. Ultimately, my calculations proved correct, for many former Soviet republics, including Azerbaijan, took a pro-Western orientation, which created a lot of opportunities for me to see the world and work in other countries. But there was a period of several months when I wondered whether my luck had run out. It had been difficult to leave Moscow; after all, I had lived and worked there for twelve years. My wife and I walked the streets, remembering our first days together, excited about the prospect of returning home where our daughter would be able to spend time with her grandparents, aunts, uncles, and cousins. So we left with light hearts, full of anticipation and hope of a newly independent country ripe with opportunity. But even as hopeful as I was about our future, my past experiences and disappointments kept me in check, and I decided not to relinquish my Moscow apartment just yet. I, of course, could not afford two apartments, one in Moscow and one in Baku, so my wife and I split up. She and my daughter lived with her parents, and I lived in my mother's home along with my brother and his family. Leila and I dared to believe the situation would be temporary and we would be reunited once I was given the promised position. My decision to hold onto my Moscow apartment was prophetic, because no sooner had we left Moscow than we encountered an unexpected problem and had our first experience with the new face of Azerbaijani corruption at that time. No longer was the corruption masked by the face of the Soviets. This time the corruption was internal, due to the forces at work within the new Azerbaijani government and diplomatic corps. The Popular Front was running the government, and after seventy-plus years of Communist rule, they were decidedly anti-Soviet.

Many of the leaders of the Popular Front resembled the thugs of Soviet Russia—they just wore different uniforms. As a sign of independence, they insisted that the populous speak only Azeri, notwithstanding the fact that for the last seventy years the citizens of the large cities in Azerbaijan spoke Russian as their primary language. To insist on immediate change was foolhardy and unnecessary.

So, while my Moscow credentials were impressive, they actually worked to my disadvantage in the nascent days of the democracy. I found myself in the offices of the foreign ministry daily. I arrived with my letter of invitation in hand and left with the same letter—promises only, but no employment. I was losing patience and was beginning to think I would have to return to Moscow. I was angry and depressed and felt foolish in believing that once the Soviets left, things would instantly change, that education and work ethic would count for something instead of money and influence. I began to consider returning to Moscow, and I almost came to blows with my father-in-law who threatened refusal in allowing Leila or my daughter to leave Baku for Moscow during this time of uncertainty.

Finally, the ice broke. I cornered Albert Aliyev, the deputy foreign minister. He had greeted me every day as I arrived to see if my position had been finalized, and he nodded when I complained to him. It seemed to me at the time that at least he was sympathetic to my situation. I called his name as he approached and stood in front of him so that he was unable to pass. I barely controlled my temper and spoke to him through gritted teeth. I wasn't sure he was listening to me, but he was clearly watching me. I started to perspire as my emotions took over, and I saw him look at my upper lip. Self-conscious, I wiped it, and he nodded—perhaps an acknowledgment that my words were true and my situation required action. Then he took my papers from me and disappeared into the building. I stood there wondering whether my precious letter was being destroyed and calculated my next course of action if in fact it was. Fortunately, I never had to prepare a plan. Aliyev returned ten minutes later and announced to me that I was now officially employed by the foreign ministry of Azerbaijan. Finally, six months after I returned home, I received my diplomatic credentials and was asked to serve as second secretary to the Ministry of Foreign Affairs of Azerbaijan.

At the foreign ministry, I was to work in the information department. Our offices were in an old building in the center of the city not far from the boulevard at the Caspian Sea. It was a simple affair. The entire department was located in one room; even the head of the department, Fakhraddin Kurbanov, shared space with us. We each were assigned a table, which served as a desk. Our duties were simply to assess and categorize the incoming and outgoing information related to our diplomatic activities with other countries. Still, I was worried that my failure to ally myself with the ruling party would once again hurt my chances for advancement. Fortunately, that did not come to fruition. Two months later, I was promoted to first secretary. We moved offices and I was appointed acting head of the press service. The Popular Front government was strongly pro-Western, so my ability to speak English and my research in Western politics became an advantage. I was placed in charge of US and Canadian affairs in the international department. Things were beginning to look up; my family's fortunes were improving.

We relinquished our Moscow apartment and moved into a spacious apartment formerly owned by the daughter of a Soviet general. My family was finally reunited under one roof. I returned briefly to Moscow to retrieve the few furnishings we had and moved them up into our second-floor "Stalinka"-style apartment, so-named after the former Soviet leader Stalin. It was a nicely designed three-room apartment with high ceilings, wide windows, and solid walls. It was located close to the center of the city, with two balconies: one facing an inner courtyard and the other facing a busy city street across from a statute of Azizbekov, one of the former Soviet Baku commissars. The statue had an outstretched hand that symbolized forward movement into the future. I loved the statue and often whispered to it, asking which way it was directing me, where should I go? My daughter started preschool. It was located right next door to our building, and I was able to walk to work. The first floor of our building housed a music school, and I have fond memories of readying for work and beginning my walk down the hill listening to the cacophony of sounds coming from the rooms below.

We spent time with our family and a small group of friends from the ministry. My closest friend was deputy foreign minister Albert Aliyev, after he forgave me for accosting him in the corridors of the ministry, and I thanked him for his efforts to help me win my appointment. He was elderly and gray-haired; he walked fast and talked the truth. He never hid his past as a former KGB colonel, even though that association was frowned upon by the ruling Popular Front. Indeed, he shared my concern that the leadership was creating an international image of incompetence and inexperience in foreign affairs.

Many ill-considered actions were taken with regard to Azerbaijan's relationship with Iran and Russia. Some people were concerned that the former Soviet government would once again invade our country and reassert its power. There were clear reasons to distrust the Iranian government as well. There are an estimated twenty million ethnic Azeris living in the northern provinces of Iran, concentrated in and around the city of Tebriz. The central Iranian government has always been suspicious of the ethnic Azeri population, and Iran was concerned that a strong, independent republic of Azerbaijan could become a powerful destabilizing factor within its borders. Nonetheless, as a small country, surrounded by big regional players, Azerbaijan could ill-afford to undertake any aggressive action at the time of our fragile independence. Those countries could cause a lot of troubles for us. And allegedly they did. After the Armenian–Azerbaijani conflict broke out, reportedly both Russia and Iran unofficially sided with Armenia. As a result, Azerbaijan lost about 20 percent of its territory: the Nagorno-Karabakh region plus seven additional surrounding regions. In my opinion, that was the price that the Popular Front of Azerbaijan paid for its clear anti–Russian and anti–Iranian policies, which was the result of a lack of political and geopolitical experiences.

In addition, I was frustrated then by the growing strength of the relationship between Azerbaijan and Turkey. The slogan among the diplomats working with Turkey was "One nation, two countries." I thought Azerbaijan had had enough of foreign influences, and it was time to continue the history and development of our own separate, independent nation. However, many years later, I realized that these strong bilateral relations between the two countries and Turkish steady support of independent Azerbaijan proved to be very important in many aspects. Nevertheless, Turkish influence partially dissipated after the Popular Front lost power, and the members of the foreign service who had championed the Turkish cause emigrated there.

As diplomats in the ministry, Aliyev and I would voice our disagreement with the government privately to each other, but we didn't dare publicly voice our disagreement. If we had, we would simply be fired. Most of the ministry employees didn't really care much about the policies conducted in this or that area; everybody was busy trying to get an assignment to one of the embassies abroad. The interdepartment intrigues were mainly aimed at who was going to be the chief of this or that department. However, in general, I believe the foreign ministry played a positive role in developing Azerbaijan's independence, and I am proud that I shared the strategic direction of the foreign ministry in the development of it.

The government was actively involved in applying for membership in strategic international organizations, including the United Nations (UN), Organization for Security and Co-operation in Europe (OSCE), and North Atlantic Treaty Organization (NATO). Foreign policy priorities included the development of peaceful diplomatic and economic relationships with neighboring countries, integration into the world economy, and the promotion and exploitation of Azerbaijan's rich oil reserves. The first attempts by the Popular Front to use oil was, in my opinion, a very powerful economic and diplomatic tool. That factor was fully utilized by the government of Heydar Aliyev, which came to power one year later. Eventually, it attracted the commercial interests and much-needed investment of Western countries in Azerbaijan, and later it influenced the strategic relationships between Azerbaijan and the West, particularly the United States. Today, the powerful oil consortium that consists of international oil companies is fully operational in the capital Baku. Not only has it had a significant influence on Azerbaijani foreign policy but also it has contributed to the beginning of the creation of an Azerbaijani middle class by opening employment opportunities to young English-speaking Azeris.

However, to date, in my opinion, not enough has been done to expand opportunities and encourage the growth of the middle class. That failure has led to increased economic difficulties and encouraged the continued growth of the black market and graft. It continues to be a corrupting force in Azerbaijan, and, I believe, in Iraq as well.

In 1992, special attention was being paid to relations with the West, and the United States in particular. As a person in charge of US and Canadian affairs, I was actively involved in different meetings and negotiations with US embassy representatives. The first US ambassador to Azerbaijan was Richard Miles, and I was in regular contact with his deputy, Robert Finn. Finn was a former Turkic language scholar. He sometimes spoke in Azeri, but with a strong Turkish accent. Actually, the Azeri and Turkish languages share much of the same vocabulary, so he was able to converse with locals in their own tongue and still be understood. We had a very good working and personal relationship; he and I usually spoke to one another in English.

By the end of 1996, Azerbaijan had become a full-fledged member of the international community. The single blot on our international status was Section 907 of the Freedom Support Act. The Freedom Support Act was legislation enacted by the United States government designed to help rebuild the newly independent republics of the former Soviet Union. Passed on October 24, 1992, it is replete with provisions for financial, technical, and other forms of assistance "to support freedom and open markets in the independent states of the former Soviet Union."[1] Amid these good works, however, is a little-known but important and mischievous clause that prohibits the provision of US assistance "to the Government of Azerbaijan until the President determines that the Government of Azerbaijan is taking demonstrable steps to cease all blockades and other offensive uses of force against Armenia and Nagorno-Karabakh."

In brief, although often seen as a religious war between Christians and Muslims, the Armenian–Azerbaijani war is really a territorial dispute over Nagorno-Karabakh, a region located in the western part of Azerbaijan. The conflict compares in many ways to the Serbian–Muslim war in Bosnia and the Sunni, Shi'ite, and Kurd conflicts in Iraq. It is a dispute that began centuries ago and, consistent with the cultural realities of Central Asia and the Middle East, has survived generations of death and destruction.

The modern face of the conflict began in February 1988, when Armenians perceived a weakness in the Soviet central government and decided to take advantage of it. Ethnic Armenians living in Nagorno-Karabakh demanded secession from Azerbaijan to join Armenia, arguing that their low status in Azerbaijan made life there intolerable.

The Armenian authorities in Yerevan then armed Armenian nationalists in Nagorno-Karabakh and sponsored the creation of a military force. From the beginning, Yerevan authorities claimed they were not involved in the fighting, insisting that the Armenians of Nagorno-Karabakh shouldered the entire military effort—an amazing contention given that its tiny population of one hundred and fifty thousand was soundly beating an Azerbaijani population of 7.5 million then. The hollowness of this claim became obvious over time. For example, the *New York Times* reported in August 1993 that the Armenian army, not forces from Nagorno-Karabakh, controlled the Azerbaijani city of Zangelan.

The war between Armenia and Azerbaijan easily ranks as one of the bloodiest conflicts among the former Soviet republics. What had been mainly local warfare during the Soviet period (1988–1991) has, since Azerbaijan claimed independence, developed into an open military conflict between two states.

Fortunately, I did not lose any family members to the conflict, but it claimed the life of a former colleague of mine from my days in Moscow. Tofig Ismailov was a man dedicated to peace. He traveled between Azerbaijan and Moscow in a vain attempt to find a solution and halt the bloodshed. He died when his helicopter was shot down during a peace mission to the region.

The official Azerbaijani position calls for an end to fighting on the basis of existing borders, the assurance of minority (namely, Armenian) rights in Nagorno-Karabakh, and the safe return of refugees to their places of permanent residence. In contrast, the Armenian side wants to keep the occupied territories under its military control.

The Nagorno-Karabakh conflict continued to play a significant role in my life. One September morning in 1992, I arrived at work and was greeted by the assistant to the foreign minister, who informed me that I was assigned to accompany a group of Western journalists to an area of war operations. It was actually one of my first assignments as acting head of the press service. There were five Western journalists in the group. I didn't particularly like them. They were interested in details but not realities. They didn't seem to understand we were about to enter a war zone where people were suffering horrible injuries and dying. Their attitude toward the locals was characterized by arrogance, but I appreciated their openness and professionalism. They were dressed very casually; some of them were wearing typical multi-pocket jackets, which they usually wore in the field. I was wearing a suit, which I came to regret later in the day. They were quite young, between twenty-five and thirty-five years old. Of the group, I learned that at least one journalist was American and one was British. I never learned the nationalities of the other three.

We were transported to the airport by minibus and then boarded a Soviet-made helicopter to the city of Aghdam. As we approached the area, the chopper began to fly in a zigzag pattern so as to avoid hostile fire from below. Twelve years later, I was to take the same type of trip into Baghdad. As soon as we started to approach the conflict area, the fellow from Britain became very aggressive, trying to record everything he saw and thrusting his upper body over the window of the helicopter. He was hanging out so far that his entire upper body was outside of the chopper, and I was afraid that he would fall. I tried to warn him, but he ignored me.

From up above, we could see lakes, mountains, and forests that had become no-go zones. I was momentarily overcome with sadness and regret, believing that this was probably the last time I would see these places. I closed my eyes and breathed in the air and tried to commit it to memory. I tried to engage the pilot in conversation, a stocky young man sporting a large moustache. He spoke little, but I did learn he was originally from Aghdam, which was under siege by Armenian forces operating out of their positions in the village of Nakhichevanik. The pilot boasted to me that the people of the city were ready to defend it to the death, but he was worried about rumors that the Armenians were receiving support from Russians and other mercenary groups. I never learned if the rumors were true.

Once we landed, we were transported by Jeep to the Azerbaijani command post. The trip took about an hour. *Aghdam* translates roughly as "white roof," and I remembered as a child being told stories about the brave people of that city. I was shocked by the state of it when we arrived. Aghdam had been a wealthy city, and its people took great pride in its appearance, but there was no longer any dignity to the place. Few people walked the garbage-filled streets. There were no rooftops on any of the houses in my field of vision. The structures resembled the jagged teeth of the monsters that populated my childhood nightmares. There was no greenery, just dust and holes and all manner of debris. Only weeks later, fearing recapture by Azerbaijan, the city was completely destroyed by Armenian troops. Today the city stands as a silent monument to the waste of war. It is a ghost town, its rich culture destroyed. It serves as a source of construction material and sullied income for the scavengers of war.

Upon arrival, we were met by one of the commanders of the Aghdam military unit. I believe he was a colonel. He looked exhausted. I introduced the journalists to him, and he introduced himself to them. We followed him past a group of young soldiers between eighteen and twenty years old. They, too, looked exhausted in their dusty uniforms, smoking cigarettes and talking quietly, their Kalashnikovs by their sides covered with green tape to keep the magazines tighter against the assault rifle. The journalists took notes as we followed the colonel toward the mobile field hospital. Before we reached the hospital, he stopped at a large, single-story building and bid us to enter. It was a warehouse. It stored the dead. This was the first such warehouse I would enter; the second one would be in Iraq. Poets, reporters, and novelists have written much about the battlefield, but no one has ever written about the warehouses of the dead. When the dead are not buried in mass graves, they are stored in warehouses. The first thing that strikes you when you enter a "dead warehouse" is the silence. Actually, it is more like an absence of sound. It's as if the sound space is dead too; there is no echo. There is not so much a chill as a lack of warmth because of a lack of body heat to warm the space. The air is heavy and damp, like breathing through a wet blanket, and there is an odor that is a mixture of mold, blood, and summer's stagnant water due in part to decay and in part to the natural release of body gases from the dead. There is no dignity or glory in such a place. The warehouse I visited in Iraq was clean and neat. But the bodies I saw in the warehouse in the Nagorno-Karabakh region of Azerbaijan were not treated as well. Most were not covered; some were sitting up, others leaning, still others lying down. They seemed animate even in death, their bloated bodies causing their clothes to stretch taut as if they ate too much at their last meal. At first, I thought all the people in the room were crouched together hiding from the war. Then the smell hit me, and I realized they were dead and apparently had been stored there for quite a while. The colonel looked at the journalists, his face had grown deep lines in it just in the few minutes since we entered the warehouse. He looked at me and gestured toward the journalists, indicating he wanted me to interpret: "Look at what is happening to ordinary citizens; what was their fault?"

I still have dreams of that place, but they are mingled now with images of my time in Iraq. My dream begins with a child standing on the roadside; he has no shoes. His dark brown hair has a gray caste of dirt, but it's his eyes that stir my soul. They are a deep brown, almost black. There is an emotion behind them, but I can't tell if it's fear or deceit. So I don't answer his pleas for help, and I return to the truck. I open the door and look in; it is not the interior of the convoy truck, black leather and army camouflage. It is the interior of a building. I slowly realize I have entered a mobile train hospital in Azerbaijan. I am cold; there is no desert heat to warm me. I step in and look around. I see gurneys lining the hallways in disarray. Doctors and nurses walk past me with clear intensity of purpose. I look down. I am still wearing my combat boots. I look up again and see the boy. He is there with a woman. She is lying on the floor, limp. Her filthy clothing drapes a frail frame. Her breathing is fast and light; it reminds me of the sound of a fluttering bird. Her hair, matted against her face, has no color. She is silent, but her body screams in pain. She is his mother. The boy is sitting on the floor, his mother's head in his lap. He takes a wet piece of hair and moves it back against his mother's scalp. Then he takes his finger and touches the curve of her eyebrow and follows the contour of her face to her chin. His mouth is slightly ajar, lips curled down. He looks at me. Now I understand. It is fear. He is crying. His mother is so small—shriveled really. A doctor shakes his head; he is speaking to me now in English, now in Russian, now in Arabic: "Nothing can be done. The boy's mother will die." I moan.

The woman of my dream is from the conflict over the Nagorno-Karabakh region. I watched her as she died in the mobile hospital we were to enter later, but the son in my dream is not her son; he is the son of another woman in Iraq. I never saw the Iraqi boy's mother; I only listened to his plea for help. I was part of a convoy in Iraq, and as we passed the boy on the road, he flagged us down and begged for help. I was the only one who understood his words, but we all understood their meaning. Nonetheless, we were under orders not to leave the road or the convoy, and under no circumstances were we to enter the homes of Iraqis that had not been previously cleared. It was too dangerous. The insurgents used any means available to mount an attack or kidnap a contractor. The kidnappers had different motives—some were political while others were purely for criminal profit, using the names of known terrorist organizations as a cover. Women, children, the sick, the elderly were used as a guise or pretext to lure us into a trap. My internal conflict never changes. Fear and death bring all characters home to me. I am still haunted by the boy's look.

The journalists' response to the warehouse was clinical. They asked questions and continued to do their jobs. We left that place and entered a train that had been converted into a mobile hospital. It was a Soviet-style train with *kupe* (separate cabin sections) and *plaskards* (open sections). If they could, the wounded sat in seats; if they couldn't, they lay down, their legs blocking the aisle and making it difficult to move from one patient to the next. It was there we saw the woman of my dream. Actually, the boy had already died, and she was dying.

The journalists asked questions about the closeness of the hospital to the frontlines and the logistics of evacuating the population. The woman sat there, her grandson in her arms, and died. That was it. It was over. Her life, his future, because of a piece of land that now serves as empty space. The journalists asked the colonel why the families had not been evacuated when the shooting started. He answered that the shelling was in fact sporadic and the families, reluctant to leave their homes and afraid of looting, believed they could wait out the latest onslaught. Some of them were obviously wrong.

The journalists moved on. The hospital was too sedate; they wanted to see where the fighting was. Despite the colonel's objections, they insisted on going to the village of Nakhichevanik. Nakhichevanik is not far from Shusha, and I told them about my connection to the place. They asked me background questions, and I gave them as much information as I could. I had no choice but to escort them there; my instructions were to take them wherever they wanted to go. We were not offered the protection of the soldiers. We were on our own, without weapons or protective gear. I was in my suit and tie. The closer we got, the louder the sounds of war became: shells exploding nearby and bullets flying overhead. We had to crawl on our hands and knees in order to avoid having our heads blown off. We were almost at the outskirts of Nakhichevanik. I could see the houses and hear the dogs barking not far in the distance. I could smell something burning, but I was not sure what it was, and I imagined the worst. My mind actually began to wander, and I thought I should have brought a knife with me so I could kill myself if I were captured. I had the same bizarre thought when I was in Iraq and we traveled through unfriendly villages. As we approached Nakhichevanik, I could see some of the houses and a chain of beautiful mountains behind the village. It was as if nature was saying, "No matter how much ugliness you bring to the world, I will always bring something beautiful before it." My gaze met the gaze of the youngest of the group, and I could read fear in his eyes. Finally, the rest of the group realized the danger of the situation and agreed to turn back. Five or six hours after we arrived in the war zone, we boarded helicopters back to Baku. On our return trip, we carried two wounded soldiers: one was young, perhaps nineteen or twenty, and the other was older, perhaps thirty. I watched their faces as we zigzagged our way back home. The older soldier looked healthier; the younger one was pale, and his breathing was shallow. He was still breathing when we disembarked. I never learned his fate, and I never forgot his face.

In March 1993, the newly appointed ambassador, Hafiz Pashayev, approached me in the ministry. Reportedly, the foreign minister and member of the Popular Front, Tofig Gasimov, recommended him to that position. Apparently, they were both physicists by profession, having met at the Azerbaijani Academy of Sciences where they had worked together. Later, they both served as top diplomatic representatives of Azerbaijan. Ambassador Pashayev talked to me several times and asked a lot of questions about my background, and knowing that my dissertation analyzed several aspects of US foreign policy, he requested a copy of it. It was clear that I was a potential candidate to go to the United States to work in the embassy, which did not exist yet. I would be part of the team that would open it. I had already participated in negotiations with the American ambassador and his staff on issues related to the Nagorno-Karabakh conflict. Clearly, the death and destruction had to stop. In addition, a solution to the problem was necessary in order to encourage much-needed investment into Azerbaijani oil and gas industries.

I was one of the few in the foreign ministry who could speak fluent English and understood US culture. Nonetheless, I was offered, and I accepted, the position of first secretary for political affairs in the soon-to-be-established embassy of Azerbaijan in the United States. The preparations began. Pashayev put together the diplomatic team who would open the first embassy in the United States to represent the new democratic republic of Azerbaijan. Pashayev's driver and bodyguard, Gahraman Mustafayev, was responsible for taking care of procedural and administrative issues relative to our departure, including securing travel and lodging. Mustafayev was also a longtime friend of Pashayev, having met at the Institute of Physics. At thirty-six (my age at the time), he reminded me of pictures I had seen of Abraham Lincoln. He was tall and had a long, thin face. He would be traveling to the States with his wife and two daughters. Our chief of administrative affairs was Mamed Veliyev; he was in charge of administrative issues in the future embassy. He also became decorator in chief, arranging for the shipment of office furniture and rugs as well as office equipment. Veliyev was the oldest member of our group. He was married and had one adopted son. The next member of our group was Farhad Balashov, a quiet, soft-spoken man in his early thirties; he had one son at the time. He was our technology department at the embassy and had his job created for him, attempting to set up the computer network for our future embassy. Fakhraddin Kurbanov, who was my chief in the information department, was appointed as the first secretary and counsel in charge of visa issues in the embassy. Kurbanov, a tall, bold, and pleasant man, was about a year older than me and had one two-year-old daughter, the same age as my daughter at the time. The last member of our group was Galib Mammadov. Mammadov, at twenty-six years old, was not an employee of our ministry; someone, I don't remember who, told me he was an active member of the Popular Front of Azerbaijan, and for that he landed the plum position of acting second secretary of the embassy. Such was the team that was put together to work in the Azerbaijani embassy in the United States. Leila and I began to pack and ready ourselves for our newest adventure. I moved between feeling as though I was living somebody else's life to feeling I was living my own, but I would soon awake from my dream and find myself in the dental lab of my youth, staring at unfinished gold teeth. Leila, who spoke no English, was giddy with excitement and left me little time to think between the hundreds of questions she asked. I felt larger than life, full of love for my country and a sense of being part of something historic. I was so hopeful, and I believed completely in our mission and the possibilities that awaited my country.

The day prior to our departure, relatives and friends gathered in our apartment for a big party. We arranged a big table in our living room, and everyone brought something to either eat or drink. We cried and laughed and ate and joked, and when we were done, we cried and ate and laughed and joked some more. Glasses were raised and toasts were made to the health and good fortune of my family. We had a great time. It was a typical warm April day when we awoke, ate breakfast, and took pictures of the apartment so that we wouldn't forget. We had very little to pack, so when we gathered with our compatriots at the foreign ministry building ready to depart, we had only five packed suitcases. Our families came by for a final farewell. My mother cried. She told me how much I reminded her of her beloved brother, who immigrated to the United States after World War II and stayed there. Finally, the time arrived, and we climbed into the bus and headed toward the airport. I realized how tired I was as I was finally able to relax after so many days and weeks of intense preparation. We arrived at the airport and checked in our luggage. It was a simple procedure, since we were proudly holding diplomatic passports, a status that saved us from tedious procedural formalities, and we boarded a flight to Moscow. The plan was to spend a night there before we proceeded on to Washington, DC. Azerbaijan was still a new country, and it was still relatively impossible to get anywhere directly from our country. All roads still lead to Moscow; it would take time before Azerbaijan was truly independent. We were going back to the place where I had spent twelve long years, and forward toward freedom.

Three hours and thirty minutes later, we landed at the Sheremetyevo airport. It was a strange feeling to come back to Moscow after being away for a while. It no longer felt familiar; it seemed to me that even the smell of the air was different. We were transported to the Rossiya Hotel, not far from Red Square in the center of the city. My mind wandered back across time; it was the same hotel where I had spent many hours with different international delegations when I was a student working as an interpreter. It had been a luxury hotel, a place where diplomats and foreign businessmen were housed, because it reflected well on the city and the country. I was stunned at its transformation. Now, only a few years later, it was filthy and roach infested. It was a moment of transformation for me too. I began to believe in the permanence of a free and independent Azerbaijan and a future that did not include the weight of Communism.

We arrived in Moscow at about dinnertime, and we were all hungry. Only a few years before, it would have been no trouble to find a decent place to eat. Now everything was shut down and closed. Finally, after walking around for a while, we found a small café and ate a simple dinner. No one slept well in the grime and filth, but we knew the accommodations were only temporary. The next day, our IT man, Farhad Balashov, and I went to the open market to each buy a business suit. When I left Baku, I only had ten dollars in my pocket, which was money I had earned back in Moscow when I worked for a Japanese company. Our salaries in the foreign ministry were very minimal, and we were being paid in the local currency, Azerbaijani manats. I do not remember the exact salary or dollar equivalent I was receiving at that time, but obviously it was not much. And, it cost approximately $200 a month to maintain quality of life for my family of three in Baku. So, when the time came to leave for the United States, I found myself without a proper suit of clothes and without the money to purchase them. Thankfully, I was able to borrow fifty dollars from a friend of mine, who was successfully engaged in business, to finance my trip to the United States. Several years later, I repaid him ten times as much, with more gratitude than I can measure.

Leila stayed with our daughter while I shopped at the market. Balashov and I found two women who were selling suits there. It was unclear if they were related, but it was very clear they wanted to sell us something. Somehow, they convinced us to follow them back to their apartment to show us additional wares. They showed us, and we purchased some suits, but they had sultrier things they offered for sale as well. As diplomats and married men with children, we declined and quickly left. We had expected to stay in Moscow only overnight, but we were delayed and spent two. Even so, there was not enough time to look up old acquaintances and friends, and I arrived and left Moscow without contacting any of them. I was on a new road. They were a wonderful part of my past, but I was focused on my future. Finally, it was time to head West. Anxious to get on our way, we got to the airport early, and in the tumult, Leila and I left our daughter's favorite Barbie doll in the hotel. Truthfully, we were more upset than our child; she was excited by the new sights and sounds around her, and obviously there was no difficulty in replacing the doll in the United States.

I spoke to the ambassador on the day of our departure from Baku. He was already in the United States and looking forward to our arrival. He had a laundry list of things we needed to accomplish—quickly. Nonetheless, we would have a few days to settle in and get acclimated. The flight was long but comfortable. I watched as we glided over water. I had to keep reminding myself that the sparkling jewels formed by the white-capped waves below belonged to the Atlantic Ocean and not to the Caspian Sea.

We stopped for refueling at Shannon Airport in Ireland. It was only an airport, and other than the language of the directional signs, not much different than the airport in Moscow, but I couldn't help thinking, "This is the first time I am stepping on the soil of a European country." If I could have, I would have scooped up a piece of that lush green land and kept it as a keepsake. I am sure if there were a machine for measuring it, the electricity bouncing between my companions and me would have registered off the scale. I know our eyes sparkled. I saw it in my wife's eyes, and her smile told me she saw it in mine. We soon reboarded and continued on our way. We slept fitfully and awoke to a night-time view of the capital city of the United States of America. I know as children we often look at streetlights and imagine they are talking to us or leading us toward a new adventure, but the streetlights of Washington, DC, that April night were truly talking to me, to all of us. They were leading us all into a new adventure. We acted like children, leaning over one another to catch a glimpse of our future, foretold, we were sure, by the coded flickering of those lights.

We landed, and the voice overhead welcomed us in English to the United States of America. We deplaned and passed through customs as part of the masses, not as elite diplomats, which was curiously comforting. We were all equal here; at that moment, no one had any greater rank than anyone else. I took the lead directing our group toward baggage claim, because I was the most fluent in English. Someone approached Leila and without a word took hold of her suitcase. She yelled for me and I came running only to find out it was one of our associates who had previously immigrated to the United States in 1979 from Iran after the Islamic revolution there. He decided to play a trick on Leila. (Obviously the new surroundings had increased his sense of freedom but had done nothing to remedy his poor sense of humor.) We were driven to an apartment building in Rockville, Maryland, where the embassy had rented apartments for us. It was near a lake and had a beautiful green park surrounding it. We arrived en masse and stood together in the lobby of the building. Our exhaustion was temporarily abated by adrenaline.

Each family waited patiently for its turn as the rental agents cheerfully directed us and offered assistance as we made our way to our separate residences. My family was settled on the 11th floor, which we liked very much. There was a wonderful view of the lake and the park from the balcony, and we were to spend many mornings and early evenings looking out and marveling at our new lives. Conveniently, there was a market close to the apartment building, and the apartment complex was located close to the Grosvenor metro station. Many of the families had small children, and none of the women were licensed to drive a car. The apartments were completely equipped with furniture and bedding, and even the refrigerator was stocked with food, awaiting our arrival. We had a good night's sleep, and the next morning, the ambassador and his councilor came to see us. The ambassador gave $100 to each family to buy some food and other necessities. He suggested that we take several days to get adapted, which we thought was a wonderful idea, and then handed me some materials to review. We spent the next week acclimating ourselves and purchasing the additional materials we needed. Leila found a tree with the image of a snake. She insisted we had arrived at the Garden of Eden. Like Adam and Eve, our home would be temporary, just over two years, but we had no intention of leaving early; in fact, we would later ask the blessing of its creator to stay.

The next week, our work started in earnest. Our first embassy was located on the seventh floor of an office building located next to the McPherson Square metro station, not far from the White House. Traveling to and from work was not difficult, and I did not yet need to purchase a car, which I could not yet afford. My office was in one of the middle rooms on the right-hand side when you enter the office suite. Accommodations were simple: I had a desk with a phone on it. On the left-hand side of the room were shelves for books and folders. The front part of the room was occupied by Mamed Veliyev, our chief of administrative affairs. There were two more rooms further down the corridor. One was the ambassador's office, another one next to it was the councilor's office, and another room was occupied by Fakhraddin Kurbanov. He was responsible for issuing visas.

Initially we did not have any secretary. Those functions were performed by Galib Mammadov, our acting second secretary. Later, we hired a lovely Filipino woman to serve in that post. The last room was located at the end of a long corridor. That housed Farhad Balashov, our IT department, such as it was. The very first day, the ambassador arranged a meeting in his office and assigned each of us a specific area of activities. I, along with the ambassador and the councilor, were assigned the task of working with Congress, the White House, and other US government agencies and nongovernmental organizations for the repeal of Section 907 of the Freedom Support Act. The Armenian lobby had a long and successful history in the United States, and that lobby was the sole reason for the adoption of the Section 907 amendment. In almost all other circumstances, humanitarian and economic measurements determine the level of US foreign aid; with regard to Azerbaijan, the measurement was political. The politics was singularly defined, and we were determined to equalize the situation. Section 907 defined Azerbaijan as an aggressor and Armenia as a victim. It was a stunning achievement by the Armenian lobby. They were able to label Azerbaijan as the aggressor, even though almost one-quarter of the territory claimed by Azerbaijan was then occupied by Armenia. The occupation by Armenian forces led to the worst humanitarian crisis in Azerbaijani history. It resulted in the displacement of more than one million Azeris, including my own extended family. These refugees received no direct US assistance because of the amendment, creating a humanitarian disaster for my country. Several senators had already indicated sensitivity to our position. Subsequently, Richard Lugar (Republican of Indiana), Terry Sanford (Democrat of North Carolina), Nancy Kassebaum (Republican of Kansas), and Mitch McConnell (Republican of Kentucky) filed a statement in opposition to the proposal:

> By imposing sanctions against a specific country in the former Soviet Union, this amendment would establish a potentially dangerous precedent of choosing sides in conflicts which have deep historical roots. Indeed, we fear that this amendment would be an invitation to consider other such provisions in which the United States is asked to side with one state, nationality group, or religious entity against another state, nationality or religious body within the former U.S.S.R.

That would be most unfortunate. We simply do not believe that the provision will have any positive effect on resolving the conflict.[2]

In 1992, when Congress approved Section 907, Azerbaijan did not have any official representation in the United States. In fact, when I began the process of contacting congresspeople, some did not even know where Azerbaijan was located on the world map. Some were surprised, not having realized that the Armenian lobby supplied all the information they had been given. Others plainly didn't care, even when we explained it was our considered belief that Russia was supplying Armenian forces. One congressman quietly listened to us as we described our country and its resources, nodding his head and replying "good" at measured intervals. It was when he nodded and replied "good" to our description of the one million refugees who were presently suffering, living under deplorable conditions in camps with poor housing, little food, and no education, that we realized we were wasting our time. Although Section 907 declared Azerbaijan must take "demonstrable steps to cease all blockades and other offensive uses of force against Armenia and Nagorno-Karabakh,"[3] the facts on the ground indicated that a blockade by Azerbaijan against Armenia was a physical impossibility. Armenia shared only one border with Azerbaijan, and that border represents significantly less than 50 percent on the Armenian perimeter. Further, supplies could not be transported between the countries—not because of a blockade but rather because of the destruction of the war. Since the start of the conflict in 1988, all railroads and highways that connected Azerbaijan with Armenia had been destroyed.

We began immediately by imitating the successful Armenian lobby: writing letters, distributing leaflets, and making phone calls to influential congressmen and women. We also initiated contact with several oil companies in the hopes of interesting them in the growing opportunities in my country. As part of the public-relations campaign, I published several articles that appeared in numerous journals detailing the situation and the Azerbaijani position. I became a member of the Middle East Studies Association (MESA), a group that describes itself as a "non-political association that fosters the study of the Middle East, promotes high standards of scholarship and teaching, and encourages public understanding of the region and its peoples through programs, publications and services that enhance education, further intellectual exchange, recognize professional distinction, and defend academic freedom."[4]

Through MESA, I participated in debates and seminars across the country. During my travels, my childhood summer home in Shusha, the hospital outside of Nakhichevanik, and the helicopter ride back to Baku played in my memory. I had to make the Americans understand the devastation of the war and the responsibilities of both parties—not just Azerbaijanis but Armenians too. I understood my efforts could affect millions of lives; closer to home, it could affect my mother, my brother, and my sister. And finally, it could have a significant impact on my daughter's future. I was determined to learn as much as I could about my new home. I studied the history of each state before I arrived there. One evening after a seminar in Durham, North Carolina, I was invited to a reception at a local restaurant. A country music band from a nearby farm was invited to play. I was sitting next to the dance area, tapping my feet and enjoying watching everyone dance. I was not familiar with country music, but I liked it. The band had just started a new set, and everyone jumped up and grabbed a partner. Once again, I was a little out of place in my suit and tie, surrounded by jeans, cowboy boots, and hats. I had no idea what they were doing, so I stayed in my seat just enjoying the show. Suddenly, the female lead singer in the band pulled me onto the dance floor into the center of the circle. I laughed and shook my head and tried to work my way back to my seat, but she would not hear it. She told me she was going to teach me the two-step, and that it was very simple to learn. The whole group was watching; I had no choice but to follow her. She was right; it was really easy to learn. At the end of the evening, one of band members placed his hat on my head and another took a Polaroid picture of me. I still have that picture; it is one of my favorites.

At one point, I was invited to participate in a debate with the deputy chief of the Armenian embassy. At the time, my title was first secretary of the Azerbaijani embassy. Paul Goble, former special assistant for Soviet nationalities in the US Department of States Bureau of Intelligence and Research, moderated. The debate generated a tremendous amount of interest among diplomats from the Caucasus and Central Asia, congressmen, and Armenian expatriates. I prepared for weeks and welcomed the assistance of Bulut Mehmandarli, one of the journalists from the Voice of America, Azerbaijani service. The room was full, and I broke into a sweat during the initial introductions. The Armenian representative had been in the United States longer than I had. His command of English was superior to mine, and the audience was decidedly in favor of the position he was advocating. But, this was a battle done on my terms. My weapons were my words; my armor was the truth. Calmly, carefully, I explained the Azerbaijani point of view to the audience: Section 907 created obstacles to the development of US economic and strategic relations with Azerbaijan. Azerbaijan held a strategic international geographic position located within Russia, Iran, and Turkey. I described the growing involvement of the United States and international oil companies in the development of Azerbaijani oil and natural gas reserves. Then the question-and-answer period began. Now my Armenian counterpart got very nervous. He became impatient with the questioners and angry at my responses, even trying to interrupt me from time to time. He kept saying that I was not right; what I was saying was not true. He obviously was not in control, a unique experience for him. The more nervous and agitated he became, the calmer I became. It was a battle of wills. I even smiled at him or the audience from time to time and delighted in his outrage and indignation. At the conclusion of the debate, Goble complimented me and called me a brave man for speaking to the largely ethnically Armenian audience. But some of the participants were not as generous and started to shout at me and call me a liar. I looked at them, smiled, and said, "Please, I am only one, and you are many. Who is going to defend me?" Somehow that diffused the tension, and if I hadn't managed to persuade them, at least they had begun to listen. We needed to convince US decision makers that the position it had taken with respect to Azerbaijan not only hurt that country but the interests of America as well. Azerbaijan was strongly pro-Western and was strategically located between Russia and Iran. Additionally, Azerbaijan was rich with oil, and the government was taking steps to exploit that natural resource. US companies had expressed strong interest in investing in Azerbaijan but were hindered by the amendment.

In that moment, in that debate, I had succeeded in my mission, and it was a sweet victory. Afterward, Azerbaijani, Turkish, and American participants of the seminar surrounded me. Bulut Mehmandarli, the journalist from the Voice of America, suggested we go to a nearby restaurant to celebrate the victory of the Azerbaijani cause, and I was the subject of several victory toasts for having "defeated the powerful Armenians." I felt like a hero because I dared to stand up to the powerful Armenian lobby with dignity and composure. It was a beginning.

Ultimately, enforcement of Section 907 of the Freedom Support Act was suspended, and the face of US–Azerbaijani relations was forever changed. Privately, life took on a sense of order. Leila stayed home with our daughter and developed a strong friendship with the wife of our IT specialist. We became friendly with many of the staff members of the congresspeople we were lobbying. I took the opportunity to develop professionally and enrolled in classes at the World Politics Institute. One of my professors was Herbert Romerstein, former head of the office to counter Soviet disinformation and a professional staff member for the United States House of Representatives, who became and has remained my closest friend. We joined our friends Patricia and Lloyd Keagan, eating and dancing at various restaurants and clubs. Patricia was the editor-in-chief of the magazine *Washington International*. Much of the material she published contained information about the activities of the foreign embassies in Washington and highlighted various cultures and customs. She frequently invited cultural attachés from the embassies of several former Soviet republics, such as Kazakhstan, Uzbekistan, and Tajikistan, to her home. At our gatherings, mainly we exchanged information about the cultures and customs of our countries and brought samplings of native dishes. Patricia used the events as a social as well as informational resource, and much of the material she published was garnered from these gatherings. We were all grateful to her, because all of the embassies represented newly independent states, and ordinary Americans still knew little about our countries and their cultures. I was not specifically a cultural attaché at the time, but because our staff was very limited in number, the ambassador asked me to take on those duties. I didn't mind; it didn't take much time and made life more interesting. Later, I became the de facto president of our group and took on the responsibility of organizing cultural activities. At the request of the Japanese embassy, I organized a photo exhibit of the Azerbaijani–Armenian conflict and generally did anything I could to educate my colleagues and the general public about my country.

Several of the embassy staff were relieved of their positions once the

Popular Front was ousted. I was relatively apolitical, so I was safe, but it was a sad realization that so little had changed while so much was different. I began to wonder then if perhaps my future lay in the United States and not in Azerbaijan.

The Popular Front Party retained control of the Azerbaijani government for barely a year. In 1993, Heydar Aliyev, former leader of the Azerbaijani branch of the KGB and leader of the country during Soviet occupation, replaced the leader of the Popular Front and regained his leadership position in Azerbaijan. Much criticism can be leveled at Aliyev, particularly with regard to his relationship with the Soviet central government, but in my opinion, he was the right leader for the time. Even today, a truly democratic Azerbaijan does not exist, but in 1993, the level of graft and corruption was stifling. There could be no movement forward, no economic development if something was not done to curb it. Aliyev had a successful history of fighting corruption as first secretary of the Central Committee of the Azerbaijani Communist Party under Leonid Brezhnev, and he continued that success as president of the newly independent country. He deserves the majority of credit for developing the oil and gas industries in Azerbaijan and stimulating growth of the economy there. But even so, Azerbaijan suffocated under the yoke of nepotism and political payola.

In 1994, trying to further develop my professional skills, I attended the Paul Nitze School of Advanced International Studies at Johns Hopkins University in Washington, DC. It was a mid-career program that gave me the opportunity to work during the day and attend classes in the evening. After my Moscow education, it was another great educational opportunity. The educational systems in the Soviet Union and the United States are actually difficult to compare. In the United States, after high school, students can choose to continue their education in college and, after taking the required amount of credits, receive their undergraduate degrees. They can then continue their education thereafter and obtain graduate or professional degrees. The system was quite different in Moscow. In the former Soviet Union, a student first had to finish primary school, which continued until the tenth grade. If the student decided to continue his or her education, she or he would move up to a university or institute for the purpose of pursuing a specific specialty. There was no concept of obtaining credits toward a degree. You simply received a grade ranging from two to five, five being the highest and two being the lowest passing grade. There was also a system called *zachet* (nongrade courses). After that, if you wanted to continue your education, you went to *aspirantura*, probably equivalent to a graduate degree program in the United States. While writing your dissertation, you worked with a scientific consultant, or *rukovoditel* (leader or guide). After defending your dissertation on that topic, you were awarded a degree called *candidat nauk* (candidate of sciences). Finally, if you wanted to receive a higher degree, you had to write another dissertation expanding upon your previous topic and defend that dissertation as well. Upon completion of the process, you would receive a *Doctor Nauk*, the degree of doctor of sciences.

In Moscow, you were required to take a lot of ideologically driven humanitarian and social sciences and subjects such as the history of Marxism and Leninism, which were not very helpful. However, some disciplines, such as foreign languages, were very well taught. At Johns Hopkins, I learned to study more independently and be more flexible in my course choices. At the University in Moscow, there was more control exercised by the administrators and a study program that left little room for exploration of topics outside your major. I took classes in the politics of foreign aid and micro and macroeconomics. I would later find that experience extremely useful. The simple fact that the students were older was a complete change from my previous educational experiences. I liked the way the classes were designed; our professors were not only academics but practitioners as well. They worked in the state department, at the Pentagon, in the CIA, and in other government and nongovernmental agencies, which gave them an opportunity to share with us their rich academic and practical experiences. One thing I simply could not get used to was that people actually brought food and drinks to class. We never could do that in Moscow; we would be punished by the teacher and expelled from the class. I remember one woman who sat in the first row next to the professor's podium. Every class she would pull out a big sandwich from her backpack and eat it. At first I expected the professor to either ask her to leave or put away the food, but he paid her no attention at all. While this might be a very acceptable practice in the United States, I would look at her with horror because where I come from, this behavior would not be tolerated. I found it quite disruptive.

As the end of my two-year commitment to the embassy approached, I asked the ambassador for an extension of time so that I could finish my coursework. His response: a firm "no." To allow me to stay would be to admit to a loss of control over my destiny. It was yet another moment of my awakening. Many things had changed, but not enough. I talked to Leila, and we decided to try and stay in the United States. I went to the World Bank and other places, trying to get a sense about a possible job situation. I talked to my contacts in the oil companies. We even looked around for an apartment to rent. We would be leaving within weeks, and I couldn't secure anything. Would I be required to become a US citizen? It was a pleasant thought, but until that moment, I had never really considered the possibility. I wasn't sure how much it would cost, and without an assured job, I could not afford the necessary fees. I had a family to consider, and I was not willing to take a gamble. So, we returned home, back to Azerbaijan. Reluctantly, we began to pack our things.

In 1995, after working in the embassy in Washington, DC, for two and half years, we returned to Baku, Azerbaijan. I resumed my work in the ministry and maintained my title as first secretary. For the first time since independence, I found myself without hope. The barely concealed system of bribery and graft still infected the government, and the bureaucracy still held the citizens in a stranglehold. The corruption inherent in the Communist system would take decades to dissipate, if it were even possible. I was always in a bad mood. From the very beginning, I tried to do my best for my country. I had very sincere motives and intentions, so when I realized that nobody really cared, it left only emptiness in my heart. My energy was spent, and my hope had vanished. I became certain I wanted to leave and pursue my future in the United States, but I wasn't sure how to accomplish that. I needed a plan—actually, I needed a job.

The author during graduation from the Soviet military school, Volgograd City (formerly Stalingrad), USSR, April 1974.

The author after graduating from the Soviet military school, Volgograd City (formerly Stalingrad), USSR, April 1974.

The author preparing for a major military exercise, Soviet military base, Kaliningrad, USSR (formerly Konigsberg, East Prussia, Germany), November 1975.

The author in the third grade, elementary school, Baku, the Soviet Socialist Republic of Azerbaijan, USSR, 1967.

The author, deputy platoon field commander (front middle), *during a military exercise in Latvia, Soviet Army, USSR, 1976.*

The author (first from left) *at the joint event of the Moscow State Institute of International Relations and the Peoples' Friendship University with Lebanese students. It was organized in solidarity with the Lebanese people, condemning Israel's military action in Lebanon in June 1982. Moscow, USSR, 1982.*

The author in the Azerbaijani traditional dress during the ethnic festival at the Peoples' Friendship University, Moscow, USSR, 1982.

After the demise of the USSR, the author helped open the first embassy of independent Azerbaijan and served as a senior diplomat, Washington, DC, 1993–1995.

The author after the country music event during his participation in a conference in Phoenix, Arizona, as a senior diplomat of the embassy of Azerbaijan in Washington, DC, 1993.

The author with his newly married wife, Moscow, Russia, USSR, December 1989.

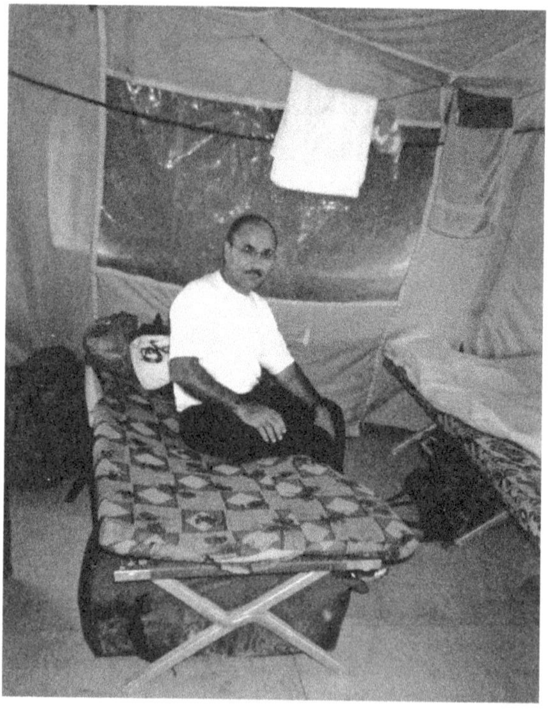

The author's first bed in a tent, Balad, Anaconda US Air Base, Iraq, April 2004.

The author (middle) with an Iraqi National Guard member and local residents of an Iraqi village during a mission with the US Civil Affairs Unit, May 2004.

The author during a mission in Iraq, June 2004.

The author with Iraqi children during a US Civil Affairs Unit mission in a local village, May 2005.

The author with his daughter at the airport upon return from his deployment in Iraq, 2005.

The author at the tent where he first stayed upon his arrival at Anaconda Air Base in Balad, Iraq, April 2004.

The author at the site of the rocket attack on the Anaconda Air Base. The attack led to many casualties among US personnel. The holes from the rocket on the ground and spots from shrapnel can be seen on the walls of the PX-BX building, June 2004, Iraq.

The author (facing camera) *at the official opening of a new school, sponsored by the US Civil Affairs Unit in a local village, Balad area, Iraq, July 2004.*

The author during the preparations for a joint mission of the US Military Intelligence and Special Forces Units to volatile Diyala Province, Iraq, May 2005.

The author at the site of the former Soviet-made planes, which belonged to Saddam Hussein's former army. Now they are stockpiled in certain places. Inside of the planes are a lot of snakes. April 2005.

The author with his daughter upon return from Iraq, 2005.

The author (right) with a member of his Civil Affairs Unit on the way to the next mission around the Balad area, Iraq, 2005.

The author (first on right) with Iraqi National Guard officers and a US Army officer during the training of the Iraqi National Guard members, Balad area, Iraq, April 2005.

The author (middle) in a Christmas family photo, December 2018.

The author (left) received this signed photo from US senator James Inhofe, chairman of the Senate Armed Services Committee, in appreciation of his service in Iraq, with the message "You're a great American, Mahir."

5

An Immigrant's Dream

I began to look around for opportunities. I approached the head of the UN mission in Azerbaijan. He met and talked to me several times and expressed a very strong interest in my skills. He verbally offered me the position of program officer, or something to that effect. I would be involved with humanitarian issues in Azerbaijan on behalf of the UN. At that time, Azerbaijan had a lot of pressing humanitarian problems because of the Azerbaijani–Armenian conflict. There were about one million refugees and internally displaced people. As a part of my job, I would keep in touch with Azerbaijani government officials and representatives of nongovernmental organizations; generally, I would act as a liaison between Azerbaijani representatives and UN officials. The proposed salary was about $600 a month, which was good money for Azerbaijan at the time. He even said that I could skip a few ranks and begin above an entry-level position. The problem was, the position required that I stay in Azerbaijan; taking the job meant I was choosing to stay. I felt as I had many years before in Baku when working in the dental clinic. I did not have enough air to breathe. I was no longer single. I couldn't take the chances I took so many years ago. I was paralyzed. I simply didn't know what to do. What's more, Leila was in the hospital. Although it was a minor surgery, I was concerned about her and entered my apartment in a fog of depression.

I am a very lucky person. I have always believed that. I understand I have put myself in positions to take advantage of opportunities, but nonetheless, when all hope seems lost, opportunities seem to miraculously present themselves. One day, I was coming back from a meeting with the head of the UN mission, which was located on a hill not far from the office of the president of Azerbaijan. I was passing a building I had passed hundreds of times before, and I noticed in a very remote fenced-in area a sign that read: "The American University in Baku." It drew my attention, and I decided to go inside and ask about it. I entered the yard and walked toward the building, which I now noticed housed several international organizations, including the Red Cross. I opened the door with the sign "American University in Baku," and I found myself at the beginning of a long corridor. I followed the corridor and entered the first door. I opened the door and was greeted by Margarita Ashrafovna, secretary to the president of the university. I told her I was interested in learning more about the university. She replied that the president was not in the office, but that I should return the following day for an appointment, which she then scheduled. The next day, I came back and met Mr. Nadir Ali Nasibov, president of the university. That day proved to an interesting turn of events in my life.

Mr. Nasibov's office was large and very comfortable. Although he was graying at the temples, he was younger than I was. We had a long and interesting conversation. I learned that the American University in Baku was the most recent of fifty-one universities to be established around the globe. This university was created only months before as a collaborative effort of the Azerbaijan-America Society and the Texas International Education Consortium (TIEC). TIEC was a private nonprofit association of thirty-two public universities in Texas that worked to develop international programs on behalf of its member universities. Specifically, the consortium was developing a comprehensive private education system in Azerbaijan based on American educational theory and tradition. I also learned that President Aliyev personally supported the initiative. He apparently agreed with the founders that this enterprise would strengthen the developing relationship between Azerbaijan and the United States. In fact, Mr. Nasibov held a government title under the office of President Aliyev and served as the editor in chief of one of the government's supported magazines. Clearly, the university needed someone with my abilities, someone who could speak Azeri and English fluently and understand the nuances of both cultures. Fortunately for me, I was among the very few in Azerbaijan who possessed those skills at that time. It was apparent during the course of our conversation that the president was interested in attracting me to their initiative. He told me they needed people like me to make it successful. They had already signed a contract with one of the educational associations in Texas for academic exchanges and the development of curriculums. Still, he questioned me about my family and political connections. He later indicated that he was considering me for one of two positions: dean or vice president. Although he could offer me the position of dean without approval from the government, if I were to choose vice president, he would need approval. Clearly, it would be easier to gain approval if he could make some strategic phone calls. Of course, I could offer him no help. Once again, I did not have a relationship with anyone in power. He did not expressly offer me either position that day, but he sent me home to think about which one I might be interested in. I left the building and went straight to the hospital to see Leila. I told her about the two options that appeared before us: A UN position in Azerbaijan or a university position. She was very pale and weak; she took my hand but did not offer her opinion. Still, it seemed clear from our conversation that she was more sympathetic to the option of the university and the position of vice president. Those were exactly my thoughts. The next day, I called Mr. Nasibov and told him my choice. He was obviously pleased with my decision and said that he would arrange a meeting with representatives of President Aliyev's office. Several days later, Mr. Nasibov and I had a meeting with Ramiz Mehdiyev, President Aliyev's chief of staff. Mr. Mehdiyev was a small man, but I was not deceived by his height. His stature in the government was large; he had been in politics all of his life, including during the Soviet regime. He was someone who demanded deference and respect. It was believed he was the second most powerful person in the country after the president himself. Many people thought that he was effectively running the country, especially after the death of president Heydar Aliyev, when his son Ilham Aliyev became president. Mr. Mehdiyev was very friendly. He told me he had heard good things about me. I knew he had spoken with Mr. Nasibov, but I wondered what other sources of information he had tapped. His questions were insightful if not a bit personal; he was clearly trying to size me up. He asked about my background and my work in the Azerbaijani embassy in the United States as well as my previous experience in Moscow during Soviet times. I realized he was pleased with my accomplishments, and I relaxed a bit. The meeting must have gone well, because two days later I was offered a job as vice president of the university. It would be my responsibility to encourage and develop relations between the university and its US partners and to further expand those relationships to include other universities, research centers, and educational institutions. I accepted the job, and during my tenure, in addition to the original thirty-two universities that were members of the consortium, we established contacts with the American University in Washington, DC, the University of Maryland, and George Washington University, among others. Our US partners were tasked with designing educational techniques and programs; the Azeris were tasked with administrative duties. The curriculum was designed to mimic the US educational system in every way, even down to the furniture in the classrooms and administrative offices.

After I accepted the position, I informed the UN mission about my decision, and then it was time to resign from the foreign ministry. I arranged a meeting with the then foreign minister Hasan Hasanov. He did not express surprise but perhaps confusion. My job at the foreign ministry was a coveted position, particularly as the country continued to open embassies across the globe. He shook my hand and told me everybody needed to go where they felt it was better to be, and he wished me the best. I finished my final assignment, which was to write a brochure for the ministry about the university, cleaned out my office, and embarked once again on a new career.

Finally, several months into my employment at the university, the president called me and said that the time had come to travel to the United States. It was to be a short trip without my family for the purpose of meeting with our US partners in Texas to inform them about the university and its goals and, if necessary, to talk more specifically about the future direction of the university. I was very excited. The president's wife and her brother were traveling with me. In the United States, our partner, Texas International Education Consortium, arranged a number of meetings with its member universities. We traveled to Austin, Houston, Nacogdoches, and other cities and towns to meet our US colleagues. We discussed specifics regarding what was needed for our existing programs and what we needed to expand them and introduce new programs. We were already planning to expand the program to include K–12. It was a very ambitious plan, and we were exploring those opportunities with the consortium.

It was an exciting time for me. I believed in what I was doing and again felt I was part of a program that would provide great benefits to the people of Azerbaijan. My presentations reflected my interest, and I developed a rapport with my audience; some even asked me to return to discuss the issues I addressed in my doctoral dissertation. One Texan asked me if I was married. When I answered "yes," he expressed regret, saying I already had energy and a down-home style; all I needed was a Texas bride. After a long day of meetings during another visit to Texas, the president of the consortium, Dr. William Franklin, invited us to join him at his country club for dinner. It was located about fifteen miles outside downtown Austin. We drove up a long driveway to a large single-story building and filed out of the car. I was in cowboy country. Everyone was once again wearing jeans and cowboy hats. Even Dr. Franklin was dressed in cowboy boots, hat, and shirt. His wife, Sonya, also wore a jean skirt and a hat. And, of course, once again I was in my suit and tie. No matter—this time I knew how to dance the two-step. We all sat at a table next to the dance floor. Dr. Franklin was dancing with his wife. I was thinking it would be fun to dance with Leila, but I was sure she wouldn't mind if I asked one of the young girls in attendance to join me. I walked up to one of the women who had greeted me when we entered and asked her to dance with me. My accent is not strong, but I clearly didn't sound like, or frankly look like, a local. She turned to her boyfriend and asked him if it was OK with him; he nodded, and we started to dance. She turned out to be a very good dancer, and we became the center of attention. The look on my new friends' faces was priceless. I think it is safe to say they had never seen an Azerbaijani dance an American iconic cowboy dance. It was a great evening, and we laughed all the way to the hotel.

When the fun was over, I sat at my desk, wrote a detailed report for Mr. Nasibov about our experience, and set forth my recommendations regarding further development of the university. There was agreement initially. The educational programs should focus on business administration and computer sciences, but we recognized the need to expand beyond a university education to primary school in order to properly convert the system from a Soviet model to an American model. It was our goal to prepare a new generation of young Azerbaijanis who could easily adapt to the new capitalist, independent Azerbaijan and profitably function in the world economy.

Some months after this trip, I again returned to the United States. My task was to set up appropriate representation of the university in the States. If all went well, I would return to the United States with my family permanently. All seemed to be going according to plan. I arrived in Washington, DC, in August 1996 and stayed for about a month. During that time, I stayed at the home of a friend who was away on vacation with his family. I met with representatives of academic and political circles. I had regular meetings with members of Congress and their staff, educating them about the university. I also arranged meetings with representatives of various foundations, seeking potential donors and sponsors of the university. I managed to arrange to have a number of articles published about the project in a wide range of magazines and newspapers, including the *Chronicle of Higher Education*, the *Washington Post*, the *Washington Times*, and *Washington International*, among others.

Finally, every evening, I drafted long reports about my activities during the day to Mr. Nasibov. When I returned to Baku at the end of August, I was met enthusiastically by the leadership of the university and the office of the president of the country. Everybody considered the trip a success, and my family was soon going back to the United States of America.

In October 1996, about a year after we had left, Leila and I returned to the United States to stay. It was actually a very difficult move. Moving to and from the United States the last time had been arranged by the embassy. This time, we were on our own.

We rented a beautiful apartment overlooking a wooded area near the Van Ness metro station in Washington, DC. We did not have a car at the time, so living near a metro station was essential, and we were able to travel to the grocery store, my daughter's school, and other locations very easily. Our apartment was on the second floor. It had only one bedroom, and that room did double duty as my office. Still, we considered ourselves lucky. We were able to firmly stand on our own feet, live comfortably, and enjoy our lives.

Upon arrival, once again our luggage was taken by a stranger, but this time it was for real. A woman approached my wife, who was busy watching our now six-year-old daughter who was energetically running around the baggage claim after a long time being confined in an airplane. Apparently, the woman's purpose was to distract my wife so that her accomplice could steal our suitcase. It contained documents (which were not replaceable) and money (which was). It was an ugly new beginning, but it didn't dampen our joy at our new future.

I began work again in the hopes of securing a bright future for Azerbaijan. Essentially, I was a lobbyist on behalf of the American University in Baku and the Academy of Sciences of Azerbaijan. It was my responsibility to meet with US congress members from appropriate committees to raise awareness about the university and hopefully garner some governmental funding similar to that which was being given to the American University in Beirut. But the American University in Beirut was the oldest US university abroad, with a long history and experienced lobbying. The American University in Baku had just been created and required a lot of networking, which was exactly what I was actively doing at the time. It was a very difficult and challenging job. My greatest achievements were bringing together different people and creating favorable conditions for cooperative projects that benefitted the academy and the university. We achieved measurable success. Most members of Congress now knew where Azerbaijan was located on the world map, knew about its pro–Western orientation, and knew about its desire to upgrade its educational system using the US system as its model. The public was being informed about our presence as well; articles about the university and its goals were published in myriad local publications. Of course, the dispute with the Armenians reared its head in this forum. When an article appeared in the *Washington Post* about the American University in Baku, the Armenians sent out a press release and purchased an ad comparing the American University in Armenia to our university.

Later in the year, I returned to Azerbaijan with a group of congressmen. Among them were former congressmen Bill Brewster, Greg Laughlin, and Jim Japman; US businessmen; representatives from academia, including the former president of one of the Texas universities; members of the Texas Education Consortium; and former politicians. They were met by the president of Azerbaijan, Heydar Aliyev; prime minister Arthur Rasizadeh; foreign minister Hasan Hasanov; and other high-ranking Azerbaijani officials and Azerbaijani business leaders. The US ambassador to Azerbaijan also participated. I moderated the conference in three languages: Azerbaijani, Russian, and English. We were able to raise funds for the university, and perhaps even more importantly, the conference gave our mission exposure, which we believed would ultimately benefit all citizens of the country. The role of the university as an effective tool to help Azerbaijan integrate into the world's economy was emphasized. The participating congressmen promised to renew efforts to repeal Section 907 of the Freedom Support Act. It appeared my diplomatic credentials were not going to waste. At the close of the conference, we went to the beautiful mountainous area called Kuba, located not far from the capital Baku. Again, the conferees were met by high-ranking officials of the region, another indication of government support for the venture, and each of the members of the delegation were presented with a small handmade carpet with an image of the region.

In February 1997, we founded the Azerbaijani-American Educational, Cultural, and Economic Center in Washington, DC. It was a nonprofit organization incorporated under the laws of the United States. I was elected president of the center, which was created for the purpose of assisting the American University in Baku with development and funding. The center's board members consisted of distinguished former senators, congressmen, academics, and politicians; the president of the Academy of Sciences of Azerbaijan; and prominent US businessmen. Our partners in Azerbaijan were the American University in Baku and the Academy of Sciences of Azerbaijan. We needed a permanent physical presence to assist with educational projects of the American University in Baku and the Academy of Sciences of Azerbaijan. Additionally, the existence of a US corporation with distinguished board members raised the prestige of our educational, cultural, and business projects, which we were trying to develop with the university in particular and with Azerbaijan as a whole. The contacts and experiences of the board members were invaluable. For example, Duncan Gray, a partner at Baker & McKenzie, a prestigious international law firm, served as coordinator of business programs and assisted the university in its different legal issues and agreements. My former professor and friend Herbert Romerstein was also on the board. Professor Don Wallace, the chairman of the International Law Institute, donated space for the Azerbaijani-American Educational, Cultural, and Economic Center at his institute in a prestigious part of Washington, DC. We met there regularly to coordinate activities of the center. I often took minutes of the meetings. The center served as a convenient tool to coordinate our activities with our US partners, especially for educational projects. The center also gave us an opportunity to expand beyond Texas universities and cooperate with other US universities, such as the American University in Washington, DC, and the University of Maryland. As part of those efforts, we sponsored two Azerbaijani students to come to the United States and study at the American University in Washington, DC. We began hiring US faculty and sending them to teach at the American University in Baku at all grade levels, from K–12 as well as university-level professors. By that time, the university had moved to a wonderful new building in Baku, which was equipped in accordance with the US educational system.

We soon placed ads in various newspapers throughout the United States seeking qualified teachers to fill positions in all grades at the university. After receiving applicants' resumes, we began the process of selection. It began with phone interviews and then personal meetings, when necessary. We sought educated applicants who possessed cultural awareness and sensitivity. We arranged for air transportation to Baku and provided educators with apartments, which we rented from local residents. For the most part, the program was successful, except for one or two incidents when the teachers for different reasons could not adapt to new conditions in Baku.

Other high-profile meetings followed in Baku. Discussions always included debates regarding strategies to overcome barriers erected by Section 907 of the Freedom Support Act. The amendment was creating insurmountable difficulties, was severely hampering the development of the university, and, more importantly, hampered the ability of Azerbaijan to operate as an effective member of the global community. Despite this, positive developments continued. For instance, Duncan Gray, the senior partner at Baker & McKenzie and our board member, approached me and asked me to serve as a consultant to his law firm regarding business interests of its clients in Azerbaijan. This moment was of personal importance to me.

Everything was going well at the American University in Baku until the relationship between the chief of staff of the president's office and the president of the university deteriorated, which ultimately led to the closure of the university. Unfortunately, the university was incorporated as an Azerbaijani legal entity, and as such, it was subject to the political intrigue that plagued the government. All those who knew better believed the university should have been incorporated in the United States and not Azerbaijan. The former US representative Richard Dale Kauzlarich made it clear he felt even the use of the word "American" in the title was improper because it was not an American entity; it was an Azerbaijani entity. In contrast, the Azerbaijani-American Educational, Cultural, and Economic Center that was founded to support the university was incorporated in the United States. Although it too disbanded after the university closed, it was never subject to any of the political shenanigans that occurred in Azerbaijan. Once again, the problem seemed to stem from the corruption and greed inherent in a society that operates pursuant to unwritten rules of family relationships, political ties, and bribery. Once one of the university's government benefactors fell out of favor, so did its government support and protection. It ultimately led to the destruction and dismantling of the university.

Our success at the university was measured by the few students who benefited from the education we had provided them. They had survived a rigorous curriculum, which required proficiency in English. In fact, when it closed, only six of the original fifty students had satisfied all of the graduation requirements. Overseas study was costly and bureaucratically challenging. Our students received all the benefits of an American diploma without ever leaving the country. They were fluent in English, were independent thinkers, and had developed a wider vision of life and of the world. It was a very sad time for me, and the last straw. Fortunately, I saw the end before it arrived and was able to secure employment. My relationship with Mr. Gray took on added importance for me. I had already begun employment with his firm as a consultant, and with the closure of the university, my responsibilities to his firm increased.

As an international consultant to Baker & McKenzie, and later King & Spalding when Mr. Gray became associated with that firm, I made regular trips to Azerbaijan, approximately once every two months, back and forth through Frankfurt, Germany, which was Mr. Gray's preferred route of travel. Our goal was to pave the way for the legal basis for privatization of the Azerbaijani economy, and we were successful in drafting a master agreement that outlined responsibilities and set goals for that process. I participated in all of the negotiations and preparations of the contracts and agreements. My role once again was to serve as a bridge between the two cultures. I helped solve different cultural and linguistic issues when they arose in the course of our meetings, and sometimes I simply translated or interpreted if it was necessary or the meeting was important enough. Mr. Gray was a good businessman and a good friend. We can attest to many successful ventures; however, the lack of governmental and business transparency and the pervading cancer of graft, bribes, and corruption frustrated us both. Corruption was in every level of society; it seemed no one was above reproach. Everybody paid bribes to everybody else: patients paid bribes to doctors and nurses; nurses and doctors paid bribes to the chief doctors at the hospitals; applicants paid bribes to institutes and universities for admittance; students paid bribes to professors for better grades. It was never-ending. This time, I knew it wasn't only the problem of individuals but of the entire social network. It was a result of the ugly heritage of the former USSR and Azerbaijan's old national problems. I now clearly understood the difference between the two cultures: in the United States, everybody was a part of a fully diversified economy. In contrast, the Azerbaijani economy relied singularly on the development of the country's oil and gas reserves. Revenues from foreign investments in those promising areas were not reaching ordinary people.

There was a huge gap between the incredibly wealthy and the incredibly poor. The small middle class was mainly composed of young English-speaking Azeris who were employed by foreign companies operating in Azerbaijan, who lived hand-to-mouth, and were able to afford the basic necessities of life but little else. The increasing refugee problem caused by the still-unresolved conflict in the Nagorno-Karabakh region only exacerbated the problem. Graft and corruption were internal affairs of the country, and foreign investors took little interest in them, but in my opinion, the problems would ultimately hamper normal development of the Azerbaijani economy as well as the activities of foreign companies and investors.

I am not naïve. I know graft and corruption exist in all societies, but in the West and in the United States, it is not the glue that holds the economy together. As in many countries, including the United States, middle-class salaries are often not high enough to cover regular living expenses. However, in Azerbaijan, middle-class people are compelled to look for dishonest means to earn money. I was even asked to pay to secure a job for my brother, an accomplished physicist. During one of my trips back to Azerbaijan, I was introduced to someone who worked in the Ministry of Internal Affairs. He had a high-level position there, and my impression was that he was a very intelligent person. When I told the ministry employee about my brother, he expressed his anger that such talented national cadres could not get good jobs. He was full of patriotism in his rhetoric, but once he had made his speech, it was clear his interest was in me, not my brother, and the wealth he believed I could share with him since I lived and worked in the United States.

The average citizen of Azerbaijan still had very limited knowledge about the West, Western culture, and Western economic values. Many still believed that to be an American meant to be a millionaire, or at least to have great wealth. As a result, particularly among youth, there was tremendous desire to leave Azerbaijan and head West. But ordinary middle- and lower-class Azeris were frustrated by their lack of funds to support a move and by increased difficulties in obtaining a visa. Only the well-educated and wealthy could leave, and they did. It was a terrible drain on society and the economy. I was embarrassed for my country and saddened by the fact that it was failing to make good use of opportunities.

During my last visit to Azerbaijan, I experienced a final insult. I left my country and closed the door, knowing the next time I would return would be as an American. One evening, after Mr. Gray and I left a restaurant with a group of our American business partners in the center of Baku, a young girl approached me and offered herself for money. She was probably fifteen or sixteen years old; I saw my young daughter in her eyes. I was so angry at the whole situation with my country that my hands were shaking. I asked her some questions, and she told me that she was a refugee from the occupied Kalbajar region of Azerbaijan. She told me her father died two years ago, and her mother was very sick. She needed money to feed her mother and herself. It was probably a lie, but I chose to believe it. I took her to McDonald's, bought some food for her and her mother, and gave her some extra money. I asked her not to offer herself to anybody anymore. Of course, I had little hope for it; I had little hope for Azerbaijan. My efforts to help Azerbaijan were premature. The country and its people needed time to grow into democracy and a free market economy. I had outgrown my home. I needed to move.

My contract with King & Spalding expired. We had completed our work. I needed a more stable job if I was going to seek US citizenship. Because of my scholarly activities, I received quick approval for my green card. It would be five more years until I could become a US citizen, and I was looking forward to it. By then, I began working at PricewaterhouseCoopers as a full-time employee.

The next logical step in the continuation of my plan was to teach language. I taught for some time at the Berlitz Language Center in Washington, DC, as an instructor in Russian, modern standard Arabic, Turkish, Azeri, and their cultures. I was gradually distancing myself from Azerbaijani issues and becoming more American. My family was too. It took me decades of searching, living, and working in different countries and cultures to finally find my place, where I was comfortable living with my family and raising my daughter. But I also realized that the very hardships and difficulties of my life had given me an opportunity to appreciate where I lived now. My daughter would never have that opportunity. And maybe that is for the better. My wife and I appreciate the positive features of American society, with its democracy and freedom. I think we have managed to get those positives across to our daughter while also protecting her from the negatives. I think we have managed to preserve and balance the positives of American culture and the positives of the Azerbaijani culture, and our daughter's behavior and values reflect that.

Sometimes I thought about the fact that I had not become an international journalist. But even though I had not become one professionally, I had written for and published in dozens of journals so I could deliver my positions and views. And my life was very interesting; I was happy. I did not regret any choices I had made. We still lived in the Van Ness area in DC, and despite it being a noisy place (garbage trucks awakened us every morning), we loved the apartment and its convenience. We had become used to the comforts of America, and it was time to realize another aspect of the American dream and buy a house. After looking for several months in both Maryland and Virginia, we walked into a house in Rockville,

Maryland, and it was love at first sight. We knew we had found our home. It had a lot of natural light inside. It was three levels, with a basement with an extra bedroom and family room. The neighborhood was quiet, with a park and soccer field across the street. The Montgomery County school system was reportedly one of the best in the entire nation. We made our offer and moved in one month later.

Fate, luck, and sheer providence brought me to Washington, DC, where I was working on the day American Airlines Flight 77 slammed into the Pentagon. I was working at PricewaterhouseCoopers on September 11, 2001. It was certainly a turning point for this country. And it was yet another turning point for me.

Shortly after the attacks, I realized that interest in Arabic language and culture was increasing. At the language centers where I taught, I saw an increase in the number of students from the FBI, the CIA, the World Bank, and other agencies and organizations. One day I was told that the American University in Washington, DC, was looking for Arabic teachers for its newly created program. I sent in my application and was invited for an interview. I passed the interview and a language test. Interestingly, the director of the resource center was ethnically Armenian and originally from the Middle East. We became good friends. In the United States, it seemed our ethnicities were not a barrier to friendship. I was offered a job as an adjunct professor of modern standard Arabic and culture. My students were young people and very eager to learn Arabic. In a short period of time, my students were able to write a simple essay in Arabic and maintain simple conversations. I had a wonderful experience working with them. Their enthusiasm gave me even more energy to teach.

Then one day I was invited to the Foreign Service Institute of the US Department of State to substitute for a teacher of the Azerbaijani language. I have never been one to pass up an opportunity. I was constantly networking and sending out my resume at that time, trying to improve my job situation. Of course, I accepted the offer and after class introduced myself to the supervisor of the instructional division that includes the Azerbaijani language, Judith Tomas. Judith is originally from Israel, and so my circle of acquaintances and friends was beginning to rival the diversity of the United Nations. From then on, I was invited to teach Azeri at the institute from time to time. I networked some more, and not much time passed before I was invited by my newest friend Emily Urevich to teach Russian. Emily, who is of Jewish origin from the former USSR, and Judith became, and have remained, close friends of mine.

Not long after I started to teach Russian at the Foreign Service Institute, Emily suggested to me that I become a full-time instructor there. She correctly pointed out it was really a much more rewarding financial situation than working part-time at both the Foreign Language Institute and the American University. I enjoyed my work at the American University and enjoyed my colleagues, so I was reluctant to leave, but I wanted to work at the Foreign Language Institute full time. So, I went out of my way to find a replacement so that my students' education at the American University would not be uninterrupted, and I changed employment once again.

In 2004, my wife, my daughter, and I finalized our applications for citizenship. The Pentagon had been repaired; plans were being made to rebuild the World Trade Center and to construct a memorial in Shanksville, Pennsylvania. Although president George W. Bush had declared "mission accomplished" in Iraq, and it appeared that the initial mission of dethroning Saddam Hussein had been accomplished, the remainder of the mission to create a secure and stable Iraq was morphing into a much more difficult assignment. There was talk of a growing need for near-native speakers of Arabic, but I wasn't looking to change jobs again. The last thing I was expecting was a call from a job recruiter. Nonetheless, when the phone rang, I answered, and when asked if I might be interested in working for the US Army in Iraq as a linguist-interpreter for Titan National Security Solutions Corp., I inexplicably said "yes."

The call lasted only ten to fifteen minutes. The recruiter was honest. Titan had, for many years, maintained a small translating division, but the events of September 11 convinced management to increase that division. By 2003, this division accounted for approximately 7 percent of its total revenue, in excess of $112 million. It would be my responsibility to assist in providing continuous 24/7 support to coalition forces. As such, I would often be required to work in excess of sixty hours per week, which included twelve-hour shifts in wartime conditions. She explained to me that I was of particular interest to Titan because of my experience and knowledge of the culture. They had already learned that my PhD dissertation was on US policy in the Middle East. They expected I would be able to conduct myself in accordance with local customs and deal unobtrusively with the local population. I admit to being easily bored, but I am not by any means a thrill seeker. I had been to a war zone before. It is ugly. It is loud. It is frightening. Under different circumstances, I would not wish to return. But I felt a passion to be helpful to my country and was looking forward to new challenges and gaining additional professional expertise. I could continue on with my nice, safe, interesting-enough teaching job. But I chose not to. My wife certainly wished I had done that, but I didn't, and the interview process began.

The process took about three months, and of the members of my recruitment class, only 10 to 15 percent ultimately passed through all the stages and were offered a job. It crossed my mind that working as a US defense contractor would fast-track my application for citizenship, and I saw nothing wrong with that. Still, I wanted to enjoy being a US citizen while I was alive. Posthumous citizenship could help my family, but it would do me little personal good. Despite that, when offered, I took the job.

6

The Real Weapon of Mass Destruction

The events in Fallujah seem to have foreshadowed the story of the entire Iraqi conflict. While the residents of Fallujah did not necessarily welcome the invasion in March 2003, they were not initially unfriendly to coalition forces, which was of course a good omen. It didn't last long. Although Fallujah was sporadically targeted by air, it had been spared the ground war. In what I believe was a misguided effort to maintain peace, approximately eight hundred and fifty members of the armed forces entered the city on April 23, 2003, and approximately one hundred and fifty of them commandeered the al-Qa'id primary school.

Fallujah, called by many "the city of mosques," is a religious city populated by a majority of Sunnis. It is extremely conservative and has reverence for the Islamic code of honor. The decline of the US relationship with the residents of Fallujah was almost inevitable. The clash of cultures and misunderstandings were predictable. US soldiers may have been briefed regarding proper behavior and the nature of Iraqi culture, but if they were, they didn't remember much of what they had been taught. Sex and family honor are intimately linked in Iraq, as they are in most Muslim countries. Relations between men and women are severely constricted. Women are protected while at the same time shunned and dismissed. Even suspicion of lack of propriety can endanger a woman. For all the repression women face, their sensibilities must be protected, and men must not parade in front of them while inappropriately dressed. Muslims are quick to find insult from the treatment of their women. It is unacceptable to take pictures of women, and they are not to be spoken to without a male escort.

Stories regarding rude behavior swept through the city and surrounding villages. Salman, my Iraqi counterpart and the man who was to become my best friend during my time there, repeated to me the stories of alleged improprieties by US soldiers to Iraqi women: soldiers sunning themselves on rooftops without shirts on in full view of women, women touched by men, homes searched while women were still in their nightgowns. When rumors spread that the soldiers used night goggles to spy on women, the inhabitants were further offended by their use. The rumors took a sinister turn, and many Iraqis came to believe the night-vision goggles enabled the soldiers to see through clothing. They started to believe that children were being detained at their schools and given bubblegum wrapped in paper that contained pornographic pictures. These incidents, some of which I am sure were accurate and others obviously fabricated, were repeated throughout Iraq, even by local imams in their sermons, so that ultimately the stories were treated as unassailable fact by the citizenry. Resentment grew. I think what sometimes gets lost in all of the rhetoric is the fact that US units are populated with individuals who are barely out of their teens. They are more boys and girls than men and women. They receive excellent combat training, but nothing can replace life's experiences. It is my belief that the youth of the soldiers played a large role in the Fallujah debacle.

After soldiers commandeered the al-Qa'id primary school, residents resented the soldiers and wanted them out. The US commanders agreed to leave, and they were packed and planning to vacate the school on April 29. On the evening of April 28, a group of approximately two hundred protestors approached the school. At this point, reports diverge.[1] Although protestors insist they were unarmed, the soldiers at the scene were equally insistent that the protesters were armed. I will leave those who are much more expert than I to determine the truth, but I too was in the army at the age of nineteen and twenty. I have spent time with these young Americans, and I am convinced that the initial violence in Fallujah could have been diffused with greater sensitivity to cultural considerations. It is undisputed that these young soldiers heard shots. It remains disputed whether or not the shots were fired at them or in celebration some distance away. It is the nature of war that young people are faced with impossible choices. They must either choose to face death by the hand of the enemy or face the enemy with death by their own hand and risk the possibility of shooting civilians. The damage created by the choice is not collateral—it is devastating. In short, the soldiers reacted as scared young people would. They fired their weapons: seventeen civilians died and more than seventy were wounded. Americans lost one of the first and most important battles for the hearts and minds of the Iraqi people. Whatever initial euphoria there may have been was lost one month into the battle. Violence steadily increased in the city.

Two days later, on April 30, the Eighty-Second Airborne Division was replaced in the city by the Third Armored Cavalry Regiment. The Third Cavalry was significantly smaller in number and chose not to occupy the same schoolhouse where the shooting had occurred two days earlier. However, on the same day, a daytime protest in front of Ba'ath Party headquarters and the mayor's office led to the death of three more protesters.

During the summer, the US Army decided to close down its last remaining base inside the city (the Ba'ath Party headquarters). At this point, the Third Cavalry had all of its forces stationed outside Fallujah in the former Ba'athist resort called Dreamland. After the May 11 surrender of the Iranian political-militant organization the Mujahedin-e-Khalq (MEK), the incoming Third Cavalry also began using the large MEK compound adjacent to Dreamland to accommodate its larger troop presence in Fallujah. Under its control, the Third Cavalry maintained no bases inside the city of Fallujah.

Approximately one year after the invasion, the city's Iraqi police and Iraqi Civil Defense Corps were unable to establish law and order. Insurgents launched many indiscriminate attacks and some on police stations in the city, killing at least twenty police officers. Beginning in early March 2004, the army's Eighty-Second Airborne Division, commanded by Major General Charles H. Swannack Jr., gave a transfer of authority of the al-Anbar province to the First Marine Expeditionary Force commanded by Lieutenant General James T. Conway.[2] Citing safety concerns, American troops completely withdrew from Fallujah. As a result, the city fell under the control of Sunni insurgents led by former members of the Iraqi army. Finally, on March 31, 2004, the insurgents overplayed their hand when they ambushed a convoy containing four American military contractors from Blackwater USA, a private security firm. The contractors—Scott Helvenston, Jerko Zovko, Wesley Batalona, and Michael Teague—were killed when grenades were thrown through the window of their car. One of the men was decapitated. Two of the charred corpses were dragged through the streets and were hung over a bridge that crossed the Euphrates River.

At the time of this event, I was in Fort Benning, Georgia, preparing for my own deployment to the region. We all knew beforehand that we would be entering a war zone, but the pictures and the description of the increasing violence were sobering. Several people decided the situation was too dangerous and opted to leave the training. I watched the television; the men swinging from ropes on the bridge were men like me. They were nonmilitary men who had gone to support the rebuilding of Iraq. There was no sense of humanity in the pictures of the dead men or in the pictures of the celebrating crowds. The crowd was a mass of contorted faces. Mouths were open and twisted; they reminded me of Halloween jack-o-lanterns: haunting but flat, the flickering light behind them providing no illumination or warmth. There were flashes of fire in some eyes, but like the flame of the jack-o-lantern, the flashes had no meaning. They were only a reaction to something external. Is it madness that overtakes such a crowd? Are we all capable of such madness? Worse, am I?

Three weeks later, I arrived on Iraqi soil. I was frightened, but I never considered quitting. I had a sense of being part of an important mission. Those of us who elected to stay did so for varying reasons. One of my colleagues decided dying in Iraq was better than dying from cancer at home; another saw glory and honor in supporting the fight for freedom. Certainly, none of us would have agreed to take on such a dangerous mission if the economic remuneration was not substantial. Money was one of the reasons I agreed to take the job, but no amount of money is worth dying for, so of course there had to be something else in it for me. I was a husband and a father and had responsibilities to my family, not to mention my desire to grow old with my wife and experience the joys of raising our child and grandchildren. I am not a doctor and was not going to heal bodies. What did I hope to do? What did I expect to give and to gain?

I searched my soul and I found the answer: God was being used in this place where civilization began as a destructive force. But I believe that if there is a God, he is a good God, and he gave me a gift, a talent to speak many languages. Just as musical artists and painters feel a need to express their gifts and share them, I too felt a need to share my gift. I have taught and continue to teach language and culture, which is very gratifying, but I felt in Iraq, I could use my talents to affect the quality of peoples' lives. Death and killing will only lead to more death and killing. Communicating between languages is more than translating words, it is also interpreting emotion and thoughts. It is the art of interpreting in which I excel. I knew I could use my talent to interpret between people of different cultures and help build bridges between them. I could not change the world alone, but I could help.

The military, the UN investigators, spy planes—they all missed it. There is a weapon of mass destruction in Iraq: God. I do not mean to speak blasphemy or to impugn any religious belief, but God has been used as a weapon of mass destruction ever since the human mind was able to grasp the concept of His existence. The insurgents and the warring tribes in Iraq are only the most recent abusers. Individual Americans are guilty as well. During one of my visits to a bunker during a mortar attack, I met a soldier who insisted the only thing that would save the Iraqis was Jesus. Words are my business, but I looked at him and was speechless. Jesus may indeed be the savior of mankind, and his return may indeed herald peace for the world, but what Iraq does not need right now is someone else's definition of God as a solution to bloodshed. The truth is, wars really aren't about God. God, in fact, is a symbol of love and peace. Wars are about power.

On April 21, 2004, I arrived in Iraq from the Rhein-Main Air Base in Germany. The flight to the air base in Balad took about four-and-a-half hours. I shared the aircraft with three Kurdish Americans, originally from the northern part of the country. They were returning home. They had each left Iraq to escape the horrors of the Hussein regime and were now returning to help rebuild their country. I relived my own life's journey that had finally led me here to Iraq.

As we were approaching Balad, the pilot announced that our landing would be delayed due to a sandstorm. One of my traveling companions, a Kurdish Sunni, became visibly upset, certain there was a more sinister reason for the delay. As I was trying to calm her fears, the captain again spoke to us, encouraging us to recall the necessary procedures for a parachute evacuation of the aircraft. At that point, my colleague took her copy of the Koran out of her backpack and began to pray.

In fact, the airplane's landing in Balad was uneventful, but that was not true of the helicopter ride to Baghdad, where I was taken to complete my registration. The chopper would bank to the left or right and quickly descend. Then, just as quickly, it would rise in altitude to avoid ground fire. I watched as a haze of concrete buildings and sand-colored highways whirled by. Soldiers stood on each side of the helicopter, focused on the terrain below, weapons at the ready. I disembarked at the former Baghdad Zoo and spent several days there. I thought that place was the perfect model for America's goal in Iraq. The zoo, once the pride of Baghdad, had at one time been the largest zoo in the Middle East, boasting more than six hundred animals and over one million visitors a year. The sanctions that followed the first Gulf War inflicted a particularly heavy toll on the zoo, and in 2002, it was closed and converted into a military base. It became part of the battleground during the 2003 invasion, and reports of the shocking condition of the animals were soon broadcast around the world. The looting that followed the invasion further damaged the structures, and many of the animals were stolen for either food or profit. Americans, with the help of various international volunteer organizations, rebuilt and reopened the zoo three months after the invasion. Having gone from ruins to rejuvenation, it was a beautiful, serene place located on the Tigris River. I thought it was a fitting place to begin my journey.

Back at the Balad base, I was assigned to the Civil Affairs Unit. This time, I was transported by jeep with two other linguists. We were asked to don civilian clothing and cover our military duffel bags with black plastic in an effort to avoid insurgents who had been attacking traffic along the road between Baghdad and Balad since the war began. There were black spots at various points along the road, scars from the ubiquitous improvised explosive devices. Logistic Support Area Anaconda, also called Balad Airbase (although it is actually located within the municipality of Yethrib) or Camp Anaconda, was huge and handles some of the world's largest military aircraft. It took about half an hour to drive around its twelve-mile perimeter. At the time, it had five cafeteria-style dining facilities, a post office, a PBX or market where residents can purchase snacks and sundries, a health clinic, two swimming pools, a gym, and a movie theater, which showed three free movies a day.

It is a truism now that, in the end, the war in Iraq is a battle for people's minds. The Civil Affairs Unit was at the forefront of that battle. My job there was to facilitate communication so that the battle could be won. The second battle of Fallujah, dubbed Phantom Fury by the US Department of Defense and later renamed Operation al-Fajr (Arabic for "dawn") by the Iraqi defense minister, took place in November 2004, a little more than six months into my tour. Operation Phantom Fury was designed to retake the city in advance of the upcoming January 2005 elections. Once again, the story returned to the struggle for power. Among Iraqis, the struggle was about who has power over land and oil. It's about how relationships are defined and regulated between men and women. It's about who gets to write the history books and who has the right to dictate societal mores and religion. No one has ever seriously argued that the United States was engaging in a religious war in Iraq, but the issue of whether or not the United States was seeking power remains unresolved. The United States government acknowledged that one of the initial justifications for the invasion was regime change.[3] Once that was accomplished, there is also little dispute that the United States had a responsibility to ensure a transition into a functioning civil and economic entity.

The insurgents, often using God, religious imagery, and even religious artifacts as their shield, claimed a holy right to expel the coalition forces from Iraq. The United States asserted its right to remain in Iraq until a stable democratic government was in place. The United States claimed to be fighting for the liberation of the people of Iraq—first from the tyranny of the Saddam Hussein regime and then from the tyranny of the insurgents.[4] The stated motives were pure, but there is little logic in the concept that you can liberate people by destroying their lives.

Operation Phantom Fury was the largest combat mission since May 2003. The battle also marked a turning point in perception of the ongoing conflict. It had become clear that it was no longer only Hussein loyalists who were opposing the coalition occupation, but there were now new and growing groups of insurgents with differing agendas who sought removal of all foreign military forces.[5] The situation on the Balad Airbase in the weeks building up to the operation was tense. Not one of the local Iraqis I spoke to believed military action in Fallujah would solve any problems at all.

Almost immediately, as the assault began, we experienced increased mortar attacks on the base—already a common occurrence. In fact, the base was affectionately called by some "Mortaritasville" because of the number of mortar attacks it received. The whole tenor of the camp changed. We all listened and watched for military medical helicopters, which had also increased dramatically. One soldier with whom I shared space in one of the hardened bunkers during an attack looked at me and simply said, "Why did we have to make it worse?"

Conversations among friends became more intimate. One time we were stuck in a bunker for a particularly long period of time, and talk turned to asking what the most important thing was for us in our lives. I participated, but mostly I listened—and interpreted. I listened to the tone of my friends' voices, to whispers and short, choked sounds. It is in between words that you find meaning. Strange friendships grew strong during those attacks; the loquacious became quiet, and others bore the pressure as if it were all in a typical day. During those times in the bunker, it was hard not to visit death, or to at least make its acquaintance, and although conversations rarely ever mentioned its presence, it was there in between the words.

After Operation Phantom Fury, it seemed to me the tenor of the entire base was less hopeful. Among those with whom I worked, it was the generally accepted opinion that the battle served as justification to the insurgents to recruit new members. When Colin Powell resigned as secretary of state, the talk in the bunkers was that there was no longer an impediment to the hardliners in the government and that battles like Fallujah would become the rule rather than the exception. Terror became a business enterprise. Not only did new Iraqi entrepreneurs traffic in stolen weapons and contraband, but kidnapping became very profitable.

Many of the kidnappings were not statements of anger or religious partisanship—they were simple commercial transactions: I take your loved one, throw a little torture in to make it look real, and you pay for their return; we are all satisfied. US contractors were particularly profitable victims. Firas, another interpreter, a Shi'ite, and a frequent coworker of mine, was caught up in the trade. He went missing from work for a couple of days, then returned after having had $10,000 removed from his savings. Salman was a Sunni. He was afraid he would not be as lucky as Firas and often prayed he would have the strength and opportunity to kill himself if he were ever abducted. Criminals and those seeking political power used the fear of American culture as a recruitment tool, and their ranks swelled. Better to die the death of a martyr and find paradise than watch as your women walk uncovered, talk to men without the protection of a chaperone, and lose their virginity by choice rather than through the sacred rite of marriage.

Suspicion and distrust shadowed the terror. I witnessed one occasion when Americans distanced themselves from local contractors, citing safety concerns. Arabic signs erupted across part of the base, warning Muslims not to enter the dining facility. It was an ill-conceived plan created by an ignorant KBR, Inc., employee.[6] The offered explanation: it was Ramadan, a time of fasting for Muslims. Clearly, it was a poorly concealed ruse. Like Christians and Jews, there are Muslims who actively practice the faith and those who don't. The contractors were working for the coalition. If they wanted to eat during Ramadan, it was no one's business but their own. True, violence increased during the holy month, but segregation failed as a social policy in the United States, and it was equally destructive in Iraq. It sometimes seemed like the United States was exporting its entire history as a democratic experiment to Iraq, complete with racism and bureaucratic inertia. The Iraqis also carried with them the baggage of history. Ba'athist propaganda and years of repression and international isolation left many Iraqis poorly educated and suspicious of foreign influences. I had conversations with many Iraqis who fervently believed the September 11 attacks had been masterminded by Washington and Israel. There was no debate or discussion. This was a truth for them. Their minds were locked; no amount of evidence could dissuade them. I remain convinced that given a chance, it is activities like those of the Civil Affairs Unit that will finally diffuse the weapon of mass destruction that is the grab for power, and, once Iraq's economy is stable and its infrastructure secure so that the government can supply its population with basic needs, there will be peace.

To that end, I spent some of my time with the military on missions whose purpose was to train Iraqis to operate and maintain facilities built by the coalition. In mid-September 2004, I worked with two American officers who spent the better part of a day explaining a fuel-distribution system to an Iraqi colonel and major who were members of the Iraqi National Guard. The system built by the Americans was quite complicated and differed greatly from the former Iraqi system. It was also important that the Iraqi army understood the vulnerabilities of the system so that they could protect stockpiled fuel deposits, which were often the target of mortar attacks. The process of educating the Iraqi military was an interesting illustration of the difficulties facing the culture. The Iraqi men were clearly interested in learning all of the intricacies of the system, but it was never clear to me where their loyalties really lay. Although they appeared at the time to be loyal to the new Iraqi army, I was sure they were just as loyal to the army under the leadership of Saddam Hussein. The colonel was a Shi'ite and the major a Sunni, and the two of them seemed to compete for the Americans' attention, each trying to prove his intelligence and bravery.

I was unique among the interpreters in Iraq. My ability to speak fluently in Arabic, English, and Turkish often made me indispensable to the transportation unit, which directed convoys of materials throughout Iraq. I was frequently asked to assist in the security screenings of independent transportation contractors. It was a job I was proud to undertake but one in which I felt an especially heavy responsibility. Few of the local and third-world nationals spoke English, and those who did did not speak fluently. I was required to translate and verify their personal information in Arabic and Turkish and convey it to the relevant US service members. There were unending horror stories of security breaches that resulted in the deaths of US military and contractors. I made every effort to ensure that the men I interviewed were, from my point of view, honest applicants. There were many times I alerted the military personnel of my suspicions, and to my knowledge, I was able to prevent these men from being hired.

The military was acutely aware of the constant danger under which the transportation contractors worked. They were obvious and all-too-easy targets. I spent many hours at military convoy staging areas talking to them and filing reports and complaints regarding their situation. Some, unfortunately, succumbed to the lure of drugs to numb the fear. Several times I was called to translate for a contractor who was obviously under the influence of a controlled substance and arrange for his transportation off of the base and to the appropriate authorities.

Suspicion and distrust between members of different ethnic groups were not resolved merely because coalition forces employed them. At the convoy staging area, a Saudi Arabian contractor, a tall man wearing a *dishdaasha* (the loose and flowing white garb of his country) and red and white *shumaagh* (headscarf) with a squared pattern on the fabric held in place with an *'iqaal* or *ra'as*, a thick black cord, began to yell obscenities—itself an odd event. He tore at his clothes and kicked at the dirt. He watched as an Iraqi contractor walked past him, creating space and avoiding the Saudi's eyes. The Saudi ran in front of the Iraqi and faced him, nose to nose, and continued to swear. A second Iraqi entered the mix and pushed the Saudi, wrestled him to the ground, and began to choke him. Finally, one of the military police arrived and tried to pull the men apart. My job: translate between the American and the combatants without further inflaming passions. There did not seem to be a specific reason for the fight, but it was assumed that the hardships of the war and ethnic and religious tensions were adding to animosity between different foreign nationals. The hatred between the two men, who knew little of one another, was palpable. Without intervention, it indeed might have been a fight to the death over nothing.

Those otherwise healthy contractors who survived insurgent attacks often sought compensation from the various companies for which they worked. In addition to Iraqi companies, there were Turkish, Pakistani, and Saudi Arabian companies supporting the war effort. There was a great deal of paperwork that was necessary to complete between and among the countries and the relevant units of the coalition forces, so that much of my time was spent assisting men in writing and filing reports in multiple languages and arranging for the return of any material that survived the attack. Some of the stories were heartbreaking. A father whose son lost his legs to an improvised explosive device (IED) came at the behest of the Turkish company his son was working for seeking to recover a truck. The evolution of the IED as a killing device, I think, will ultimately become the symbol of this war. These weapons inspired terror by reason of their unpredictability and difficulty to locate and eliminate. The attack on this man's son occurred on a bridge near the city of Samarra; there were a lot of insurgent activities there. Even in the unlikely event the truck was still there, it was too dangerous for our troops to risk recovery.

Another time, an elderly man, or perhaps just a prematurely aged man, came into my office; his hands were shaking, and he had trouble meeting my gaze. His was the only truck of four that was able to make it to the base following an insurgent attack two months before. Two of his companions were stabbed and killed during the attack. He too sought recovery of the remaining truck so that he could bring it back to Turkey, a trip he looked too feeble and frightened to make. Still another man needed to complete paperwork confirming that his truck was attacked, leaving his partner dead. It was important that his paperwork was completed properly; without it, he would not receive compensation from the Turkish company for his work or his injuries.

Independent, nonmilitary commercial contractors have long been part of the landscape of military operations by the United States and others. But the conflict in Iraq represents a sort of paradigm shift given the voluntary nature of the armed forces and the level of reliance upon commercial contractors. According to Peter W. Singer, author of *Corporate Warriors: The Rise of the Privatized Military Industry*,[7] at the end of the Gulf War, there was about one contractor to every one hundred soldiers. By 2003, the ratio increased to one contractor to every ten soldiers. The nonmilitary transportation contractors were generally from Iraq, Saudi Arabia, Pakistan, and Turkey. Difficulty communicating among and between them was only part of the challenge. Culturally and ethnically, they were different.

My studies in Middle Eastern politics and culture were invaluable to me when trying to interpret and resolve confusion and disputes between these people. There was one instance where a Kurdish contractor's truck had broken down somewhere near the base in Balad; he needed a ride on another convoy headed to Turkey, where the company he worked for was located. My job was to explain the situation in English to the commander, relay it back to the Kurd in Arabic, and then arrange for the transport in Turkish. At other times, I was required to serve not only as an interpreter but also as a referee. There were countless "international skirmishes" among the Iraqis and third-world nationals. Tempers would flare, and objects would start flying. One time an Iraqi contractor stole a driver's manifest from a Turkish contractor and demanded a ransom for its return. Calming these gentlemen down was an on-site lesson in international diplomacy.

The health care many of the noncoalition contractors received in their country of origin was not up to the standard of American care, and many became horribly ill. One time, during the second Fallujah offensive, when danger to the convoys was especially acute, a Turkish contractor entered the base. He was pale and disheveled. His clothes were filthy and his walk unsteady. I was called immediately to assist in interpretation. The man's speech was slurred, and it was very difficult to understand him. Finally, I was able to learn that he had been sitting in the cabin of his truck without moving for three days, afraid to leave because of the fighting. At one point, he quickly turned from me and ran toward a medic. He ripped his shirt open and revealed a wet, red rash. He became quite agitated and began to run toward several people, attempting to touch them. One soldier aimed his weapon at the man as I yelled at both men to calm down, first in English, then in Turkish, and finally in Arabic. Upon seeing the weapon, the contractor stopped in his tracks. A medic was able to put on gloves and examine the man. Unfortunately, because it was not a life-threatening injury, there was little the medic could do. He thought it was probably an allergic reaction to an insect bite. We quarantined the man in an outdoor station while I arranged with some other Turkish contractors to transport the poor man back home.

The situation regarding life-threatening or combat-related injuries was quite different. Americans, true to the values of their culture and faith, treated the injuries of all who were wounded. I spent innumerable hours in military hospitals on base assisting medical personnel. Often, Americans, Iraqi military, and insurgents would be recovering in the same room. It was not always a comfortable situation. Salman, who was a local Iraqi Sunni from Taji and was contracted as an interpreter by the US Army, was always in awe of the American ethic. He once turned to me and remarked, "Life is so precious to Americans. Iraqis would let an enemy die, but Americans work to save them." It is true. It is one more reason why, when asked, I desperately wanted to answer, "I am an American."

One evening, I was called to the military hospital to help in communicating with one of the Turkish contractors wounded on his way to Anaconda base. He was wounded as the result of the explosion of an IED, suffering injuries to his right arm and side. The hospital at that time was no more than a tent. As I entered, I saw only one US soldier; most of the wounded were Iraqis and Turkish contractors. Some of them were slightly wounded, others more severely. The nurse explained to me that some of the men were Iraqi National Guardsmen and policemen. In the same room were insurgents; they were receiving medical treatment for various degrees of injuries they suffered while fighting coalition forces.

I noticed one of the insurgents was sleeping. Both of his legs were bandaged above the knees. The nurse explained that he lost his legs because the device he was setting up on the road exploded prematurely. I turned around in order to assist one of the medics with one of the Turkish contractors. Later, I noticed that the insurgent was awake and looking at me.

His eyes were large, his stare unblinking. I wasn't sure if it was hatred or fear. I questioned the nurse, and she told me that he had been quiet since entering their care, and he had refused talk to anyone. According to the nurse, once he was strong enough, he would be interrogated and subsequently jailed. I looked at him. Even if he survived, he would never again be strong. In his world, he was ruined and probably better off dead.

Participants in war have always invented nicknames for their enemies, and in this war, insurgents were often called "hajji." For Muslims, the term *hajji* is used to describe a person who has made the hajj, the pilgrimage to Mecca. The soldiers use the word *hajji* to refer to insurgents. It is a derogatory phrase, the same way the word *gook* was during the Vietnam War. It is a way of demystifying and dehumanizing the enemy and perhaps diminishing some of the terror. The military police officer, a young, handsome man who was guarding the quiet insurgent, turned to me and said, "Those hajjis are all cowards. An IED is a coward's weapon. I don't see why we don't just let them all die." I don't blame him. I already knew many soldiers who had lost friends; I assumed he had too. I don't know how I would feel in his place.

Soldier of Languages and Cultures

The medical checkup was extensive. In addition to the usual blood and heart tests, I had to submit to very sensitive hearing tests. I guess the thought was, if I was going to translate, I needed to hear what the parties were saying. In any event, I passed. The tests were conducted at an ordinary-looking two-story facility in Maryland or Virginia somewhere. I was transported there by bus with a number of other applicants. All of the others were also seeking positions as interpreters. There was one woman who I am sure was hired as a Russian interpreter, or if she wasn't, she should have been. She was American, blonde, blue-eyed, very pretty, and very much admired by the younger men in the room. They were flirting with her mercilessly.

During a discussion with one of her suitors, I heard her mention that she spoke fluent Russian. I decided to test her myself and said a few words to her in my second tongue. I have never in my life met anyone who was not a native speaker of a language speak the language so well. She was indeed fluent and had no trace of any kind of accent other than native Russian. Much to the chagrin of the younger, unattached men in the room, we spent the entire waiting period deep in conversation.

The first medical checkup was followed by a second check and a series of immunizations. This was the first time I started to have second thoughts. I felt like a pincushion. As to the security check, well, I like spy novels as much as the next guy, so when it came time for the interview, I had visions of men in gray suits with skinny lapels and the narrow black silk neckties popular in the 1960s and wearing dark sunglasses. Indeed, the interview was conducted by three men, but they weren't dressed in suits. They weren't even dressed in gray, and none of them wore a tie. Once again, I was the only one in the group dressed in formal business attire. Only one fellow wore glasses; they were suspiciously tinted though. The men were dressed in casual button-down shirts and well-ironed khaki or brown slacks. There was a large wooden desk in the room, and they sat behind it. I sat in front of the desk, but there was no stereotypical single light swinging from the ceiling. The room was comfortable, not airless. It was, in a word, nonthreatening. The men rose from their chairs as I entered, and they each shook my hand. The interview lasted about an hour, and they asked me what I would expect to be asked if I was applying for a job that required security clearance. But it wasn't a tense situation; it was actually quite friendly.

The only reservations I had were for my wife and daughter. My daughter was only thirteen at the time, entering into a time of great tumult in her own life, and I wanted to be part of it and share the obvious oncoming rollercoaster with her. She is an American teen with all the images that brings to mind, and I wanted to be part of the story she would be writing. Leila was frightened and had visions of military personnel knocking on our door, bringing her news of my death. In an effort to keep our daughter unaware, I found her one afternoon sobbing in our closet. We talked, and I explained to her my depth of feeling for the place we now called home, how I felt a deep sense of gratitude for the opportunities the United States gave to its citizens. I recalled the 1990 invasion of Baku by Soviet forces to enact a rebellion based only on the people's desire to choose their own destiny, to speak their mind, to travel as they wish within and outside of the country. We talked about Shahidlar Hiyabani, the cemetery in Baku where the martyrs of that rebellion were buried. There are no such cemeteries in the United States—there are cemeteries of heroes but not martyrs.

The invasion happened in January 1990. I was working in Moscow for the USSR Red Cross. After weeks of demonstrations, Azerbaijanis peacefully gathered in Baku to demand sovereignty and an end to the Communist regime. In response, the Kremlin declared a state of emergency and sent tanks into the city. The attacks were ruthless; anyone caught between the crosshairs of the Soviet military machine was murdered. Official estimates are that one hundred and thirty people died, and more than seven hundred were injured. Unofficial estimates are much higher. Gorbachev has since acknowledged that his actions then were a mistake, but the incident remains burned into the collective memories of Azerbaijanis. Even today, the invasion is commemorated every year on January 20, when millions of people gather at the Alley of Martyrs in Baku, a hilltop park where the victims of "Black January" are buried. Although my wife and I were in Moscow, we watched televised reports of the invasion; however, the state-run news organizations presented an antiseptic version of the truth. The purpose of the broadcast was to parade the strength of the military; they failed to reveal the carnage. We later learned from our families of the death and destruction. The United States has certainly wrestled with issues of civil rights and racism, but they were a result of internal disputes and the definition of freedom that had been written into the Constitution. The openness with which Americans reprimand themselves is sometimes ridiculed outside its borders, but for those of us who grew up in societies where you dared not ridicule, it is nothing short of stunning. Given the opportunity, how could I not choose to do what I could to defend this part of the American dream against those who sought to destroy it? Perhaps I could even have a hand in winning the hearts and minds of Iraqis. After all, I understood the repression under which they had lived and the possibilities that lay before them. I could speak to them in their tongue. This time, I wanted to take a more active role. My efforts to support freedom and democracy are singular and personal, and I truly believe I have done this in my own way, person by person. I know it sounds puerile, and I knew I would not be able to turn the tide and affect major change. But you never know who you might meet and what you can do unless you actually make the attempt. I could not miss this opportunity. Leila reluctantly agreed.

7

Clash of Cultures and Casualties of War

The Iraqis often felt Americans were not only killing their bodies but also their souls, and the death of the soul is far more dangerous. Iraqis often turned to traditional values and fundamentalist precepts as a protection against perceived US incursions. The Arab version of the ugly American arrived with the troops. Even simple interpersonal details have been overlooked. Iraqis require less interpersonal space between themselves and others; they touch a great deal when they talk. It is insulting to them when Americans step back. These are simple details that create trust and help build friendships, yet they were often ignored. Iraqi culture requires very rigid rules of social interaction. The need to maintain honor governs all relationships. In Muslim cultures, death is preferable to a loss of honor. Such cultural restraints are anathema to Americans.

As an example, one friend of mine positively broke out in a sweat every time he was required to accept a gift or join an Iraqi at a meal. He found it nearly impossible to remember to use only his right hand at the table; the left hand is considered indecent as it is supposed to be used for personal hygiene. He would tie a string around his wrist as a reminder. Of course, there were rules regarding interaction with women to which the Iraqi men were particularly sensitive. Although women's roles are expanding in Iraq, they are still treated, according to Western standards, as second-class citizens, and they are expected to remain secluded and out of sight to all but members of their family. I frequently advised the younger men to avoid talking to an unaccompanied woman. Americans also had to be reminded that photography was often viewed with suspicion by fundamentalist Muslims. Some Muslims believe that photographs imitate the creative act of Allah and are therefore forbidden. So, before taking a picture of an Iraqi, it is required for the photographer to obtain the permission of the subject.

The directness with which Americans conduct business is insulting to Iraqis, who require some exchange of pleasantries before they begin. If an Iraqi senses you are impatient and wish to "get down to business" before the appropriate conversational starters have ended, the likelihood of a pleasant and productive exchange will be severely handicapped. Perhaps most important is a cultural reluctance to accept criticism. Translating criticism without seeming critical is dicey. The complexities of renovating and rebuilding Iraq with an eye toward eventual Iraqi autonomy necessarily involved the cooperation of many parties. It is to be expected that there would be some errors and misunderstandings, but when there is a reluctance on the part of one party to take responsibility for any errors, you have a problem. Add to that an almost nonexistent legal system, a weak economy, and a strong black-market economy that rewards graft and corruption, and you have an even bigger problem.

I clearly remember one village where the Civil Affairs Unit managed the construction of a water purification plant. A local translator and my friend Salman estimated the actual cost of the project was probably $30,000 to $35,000. However, at that stage, the plant had already cost the United States $120,000. In another village, the contractors who were building the water purification plant complained that they had not been paid. The city council was responsible for payment, and US invoices indicated $80,000 had been forwarded to the council. I do not know how that particular dispute was resolved, but having witnessed countless meetings of finger pointing, I can imagine it wasn't pretty.

Although I was primarily assigned to the Civil Affairs Unit, as time went on, I found myself also working for the Transportation Unit, Special Forces, Intelligence, and the Medical Unit. LSA Anaconda–then a large US base near Balad air base (and the US facility Joint Base Balad) that spread over fifteen square miles–provides logistics support to the entire

Iraqi combat zone. Military and contractor convoys crisscross the country, transporting weapons, soldiers, and supplies.

Civilian Iraqis and third-world nationals from Turkey and neighboring Arab countries supported many of the supply convoys, and most of the drivers did not speak English. As a result, there was often a great deal of confusion and heated exchanges. Shortly after I arrived on base, I spoke to Major Blue, then commander of the Transportation Unit, and we decided there ought to be signs around the base to provide the contractors with essential information and create an atmosphere of cooperation and friendship. I designed signs in Arabic and Turkish so that upon entering the base, contractors were welcomed and thanked for their assistance in rebuilding Iraq. Other signs served as directional indicators and warnings not to enter certain areas and to refrain from smoking or taking pictures. But all of our efforts to create positive relationships seemed lost in the battles around us.

It was always hard to get a clear read on the motives of many of the local and third-world nationals working for the coalition forces. Contractors seemed to belong to one of two mutually exclusive groups: those who harbored dual loyalties and those who didn't. Those who had a single loyalty were spies and conspirators. And loyalties changed.

Friends became enemies at the drop of a bomb. It seems the lessons of Vietnam were not learned, or at least not learned well.[1] Bombs may be smarter than they were thirty or forty years ago, but even smart bombs kill innocent people. Revenge killings are part of the culture in Iraq and many other countries of the Middle East. Forgiveness is not part of the equation. Enmity is inherited by future generations as is dark hair and black eyes.

On the other hand, contractors were gainfully employed. They were making money and were able to take care of their families. That was the good news. The bad news: many of them expressed the belief that America was an invading power not really interested in nation-building. And despite all the work we did in Civil Affairs, that was the perception of many of the native Iraqis. At one point, I was translating between a Kuwaiti, an Egyptian, a Palestinian, and an Iraqi. Each of them was employed either directly by the US government or by a US corporation. There was no support among them for a return of the Saddam Hussein regime, yet in their opinion, the danger and the suffering of the general population had increased since the US invasion. The contactors were all preparing to join the military convoy in a project of rebuilding. Nonetheless, they each expressed the belief that America was in it for oil profits. Translated: it wasn't about nation-building or democracy or peace. As far as these contractors were concerned, it was about power. How could they be part of a process and yet deny its existence? Clearly the locals and third-party nationals were having a hard time hearing the American message over the din of fighter planes and tanks.

How Beautiful This Country Could Be

I stood there looking at the moon. I don't remember what I was thinking; probably nothing. It had been a long day. My friend Salman walked up to me quietly.

"When the moon is full and it is surrounded by three colored rings, it is a sign—an invitation to rain," he said.

There was poetry and mystery in his voice, and I will forever think of Salman when the moon invites the clouds to rain. Salman was with me in our bunker many times. He and our comrade sergeant Pavel Rodionov and I had become good friends. We were any unlikely group. Salman was an Iraqi. He is, by Iraqi standards, an educated man, a practicing Sunni Muslim in his mid-thirties of medium height who is athletically built. Pavel was a kid. He was about twenty, not much older than my daughter, Russian Orthodox, and had only a high school diploma. Pavel had immigrated to the United States from Russia when he was eight years old, and he spoke fluent Russian, the language in which we conversed most of the time. He was a big kid, over six feet tall with light hair and blue eyes. I was forty-eight and, at the time, still a citizen of Azerbaijan, although my paperwork to become an American citizen was complete, and I was merely awaiting the privilege to take my oath of citizenship.

In contrast to Pavel, I am smaller in stature. Some might describe me as stocky, and due to the strong Iraqi sun, I am darker in complexion. Unlike the other men, I am well educated and do not practice any organized faith, although my family is historically Shi'ite Muslim. Pavel often provided security support on our missions, and Salman assisted in translations. I was the elder statesman of the group. In Azerbaijan, we refer to the head of the family as *Agh Sakkal*, literally meaning "white beard." The Agh Sakkal is the individual to whom the family turns for approval of all major decisions. My life's experiences and education made it a natural place for me within our friendship. I enjoyed my role and felt especially content when I was able to provide my friends with direction and advice regarding significant aspects of their lives. Indeed, since returning home, Pavel has begun college studies, and Salman was seeking to immigrate to the United States.

Salman took to calling me *genius* along with many others on the base. It was a term of affection and respect that I had earned by reason of my ability to interpret in multiple languages. In fact, Newsreel Anaconda even produced a video about my work. The newsreel was one of several media outlets that chose to shine a spotlight on me. Salman would often point to my bedroom door, on which my name was printed in rather large letters, and say, "Here is the big genius. I am the little genius." And he was. Salman was very adept at translating between English and Arabic, even though he was not formally trained in the art of translation and interpretation.

Salman, Pavel, and I shared many meals together and would greet each other with the phrase "wakh, wakh, wakh." It's a derivation of a phrase I created that is used by people in the Republic of Georgia, another former Soviet satellite state. It does not translate well, but it can be interpreted as an emotional greeting of welcome. Salman and I worked well together, often finishing each other's phrases. I am sure Pavel and I owe him our lives. Salman lived in Taji, about an hour's drive from the base, so he was very familiar with the surrounding area. He knew which villages were predisposed to be welcoming and friendly and which were not, so he was able to guide and direct our travels and provide additional direction regarding our safety and security. Salman had a clear understanding of the goals of the occupation but recognized the frequent failure of implementation. It was a truth for him that in some ways, life was easier and safer under Saddam Hussein, yet Salman believed in the stated mission of the United States. He did not appear to have suffered under the Hussein regime. He nonetheless clearly hoped for a more open and democratic culture. His hopes seemed to diminish, however, with each reported death of a coalition fighter or his countrymen.

Salman was very sensitive to the delicate balance that he had to maintain. Local translators were paid well according to Iraqi standards. For most, it was the highest salary they had ever earned, but at times, it seemed as though there was no way to adequately protect them, particularly as they commuted back and forth between their villages and the base. Salman was fiercely protective of his family, but his job with the coalition forces put them and him in danger daily. He frequently said to me, "I don't talk about my job at home. It is not safe for my neighbors to know my job. If I don't talk, no one is going to know."

Death's cousins are terror and fear. They were diseases that spread through Iraq, leaving human remains in their path. We made attempts at humanity. Friendships were born, and they flourished for a while, but the disease eventually found them. Salman was my best friend for a year. We shared meals and missions, we spoke about our families, played soccer together, yet I don't know anything about his past or his present. The future is too frightening and the past too dangerous. Either may reveal an element of character or choice that one would rather keep hidden. Friendships are difficult for Iraqis. During the Hussein regime, the party and the security forces watched the creation and destruction of relationships.

Now it is old friends and neighbors who watch. So, although he was my best friend, I never asked Salman about his life during the regime, and he never offered any information about it. The disease withered any future possibilities of friendship too. Our friendship could only be in the moment and only when we were together working. He invited me to his home. I could not go. It was too dangerous for me and for him. My last day in Iraq was the last day of our friendship. We did not exchange addresses or phone numbers. That simple exchange could be used as evidence to support a contract of death for Salman. As for me, I have great affection for Salman, and I think of him often. But I, too, am afraid. I am an American now; I value my citizenship and I love my country. I am not a practicing Muslim, but I am a Muslim. I speak Arabic, and I spent time in Iraq. Contact between myself and an Iraqi is dangerous for me. To survive, to protect myself, to keep Salman safe, I can only remember him and our friendship and look forward to the day when we meet on the soil of freedom.

8

Rising with Hope from Ashes

I was sleeping the deep dreamless sleep of absolute exhaustion. I never heard the explosion or the warning siren, never had the chance to ignore it. I just slept. I didn't hear the second explosion either. Another soldier did. She had been making a phone call across the street. She saw the sergeant—shrapnel slicing across his throat and almost severing his head. She ran to him, swallowed her vomit and her fear, and pretended to be a nurse so he could die in a woman's arms, listening to soft whispers of hope. Death strikes with utter randomness in Iraq. I had intended to purchase some toothpaste at the PBX, the site of the explosion, when the attack occurred. I wasn't there because I had fallen asleep. I didn't know the other four soldiers who died that day or any of the twenty-five who were wounded. I don't know where they are now or what happened to them.

The one thing I know for sure is that the only reason I wasn't there when the explosion went off was because my fairy godmother sprinkled fairy dust in my eyes and put me to bed. My father's death came to me in whispers, but the language of the dead in Iraq is deafening. Their demands are exacting: Find them. Identify them. Return them to their homes. I heard their commands and followed their orders. Early in my tour, I was asked to help identify three men who had been beheaded. Whatever their crime, they did not deserve such punishment. Even when the heads are discovered with the bodies, they cannot be used as a means of identification; the loss of blood distorts the features, and there is nothing human left.

Tattoos, however, remain unchanged. They were in Arabic, so someone had to interpret them, and I was chosen.

They were not Turks, as had been supposed by one of the commanders on the base. They were Kurds. Their tattoos were in Arabic, not Turkish. They were verses from the Koran. They no longer served as statements of political and ethnic affiliation but insignias of defiance or hope, depending on your point of view. What made me different from those who would commit such atrocities against another person? How could I distinguish myself from them? I don't know; I keep trying to understand how to distinguish myself.

In Iraq, death is ordinary, and death is as commonplace as cancer: it invades all spaces of time and mind. It haunts dreams. Typical, even rational, fears go into hyperdrive. The few times my friend Salman was late to meet, I was sure he had perished. My wife worried that a game of soccer on the base would leave me dead. Even my own severe stomach illness was, I was certain, my own ticket to death.

There is an office in a removed corner of the base devoted exclusively to the paperwork of death. Bodies are kept in one location for no longer than twelve hours. The paperwork for Americans is in English; the paperwork for Iraqis and Turks is not. Someone needs to translate it. These men, too, demand identification and some dignity. They, too, need to be sent home. The paperwork of business continued despite the death of the courier. A Turkish contractor killed by a roadside bomb left his unfinished business bloodied. The transport papers needed translation. They were covered in blood. Unthinking, I picked them up, forgetting to put gloves on, searching the paper for anything identifiable to make him human. There was nothing.

Fear did not acknowledge rank or experience. Men who had served in multiple areas of military operations were alarmed by the disintegrating situation in Iraq. At various times, when security appeared particularly shaky, large group gatherings were discouraged. People were told to eat in shifts or take their food outside of the dining hall and eat in their rooms. Cell phones became contraband. At one point, I was asked to assist in interrogating a man who had entered the base with a compass hidden in his wallet. He claimed innocence, but in a previous incident at another base, an insurgent had used just such a means to draft detailed maps, which were then used to launch an incursion. Security was measured in relative terms. One village near the Balad base received assistance from the Civil Affairs Unit of the army to rebuild a school.

When the villagers complained that they received threatening letters from insurgents, the police chief responded by saying the area was safe compared to other regions of Iraq. My job was to translate comfort into those words. I failed. On September 11, 2001, Americans experienced the overwhelming sense that their homeland was in danger. The Iraqis live with that danger every day. Many of them do not know what face that danger has or how it speaks, what faith it follows, or what country it originates from, but it is palpable, and it is with them every hour of every day. Each trip off the base became an exercise in faith and hope.

Despite that, my favorite experiences were in the villages. Their layout, even their smell, reminded me of the rural areas of Azerbaijan in my youth. Our trips always began with a briefing led by the commander of the Civil Affairs Unit and included a general discussion of the villages we would be visiting, the length of the trip, and the status of the projects we were inspecting. Always there was a discussion of the necessary security measures that we would need to take. Some villages were known to be hostile and others friendly, but nowhere was truly secure, and merely taking the trip off the base was dangerous.

Our comings and goings from the base were often rerouted at the last minute due to the discovery of an improvised explosive device (IED) or security breach. I actually felt safer at those times, knowing the danger had been identified and we were taking steps to avoid it. I was never quite sure how that assessment had been made, perhaps by air reconnaissance or observations of material that had suddenly appeared in the daylight. IEDs might be assumed to be hidden under a freshly dug mound of dirt, a carelessly thrown can of soda, a box, an abandoned car, or a spent artillery shell. IEDs were placed in the path of the convoys under the cover of night. The safer days followed the colder nights; it seemed even insurgents preferred not to work in the cold. For some reason, although I was cautious and alert, I was never really frightened. However, on one trip, I was especially sensitive to the danger ahead.

Our mission one day was to visit two schools in the Diyala Province that were being renovated under the guidance of the Civil Affairs Unit. The

Diyala Province, located northeast of Baghdad, was then, and remains today, one of the most volatile provinces in Iraq. The province, approximately the size of Connecticut, was home to a half dozen or so jihadist and Sunni nationalist groups. It is resource rich, with fertile farmland landscaped with orange and date groves and irrigation canals supported by the Tigris River. The Tigris River and the general climate provide Diyala with abundant water. Untapped oil reserves make the province economically viable as well. Unfortunately, Diyala also supports strategic roads that connect it to Baghdad to the south and Iran to the east, providing easy access to the strongholds of all of the insurgent groups that use the province as a staging ground for their political and religious battles.

Another interpreter, Eva, was originally scheduled for the mission, but she was a Christian Arab from the province. Working for the coalition was an act of defiance for Eva. She chafed at the restraints imposed upon women by the conservative Muslim sects, but she was not foolhardy, and working in an area where she was recognizable not only endangered her safety but the safety of her family. She had already been shot and wounded by unknown assailants, and she did not wish to repeat the experience. I liked Eva. She had a desire to grow, to experience life outside of her small town, and to travel the world. She was passionate in her support of the invasion and was not looking forward to the time when the Americans would leave. She was afraid that the few strides women had made during the occupation would be lost when no Americans remained. Her dream of Iraq included her as a full and participating member; her nightmare was a theocratic government where she would be forced to become an anonymous ghost hiding behind a chador. We had an extra cadre of security for this trip, including one American, one Brit, one Aussie, and two athletic-looking security contractors from South Africa who had been employed in special police forces in their country of origin. Before going outside the base, the men locked and loaded their weapons. I sat quietly in the Humvee and listened to the ammo click into place. I felt a slight shudder; a quick slideshow of my life passed before my eyes. I took a deep breath and settled in for the ride. We were all hyper alert, looking out the windows for odd shadows or objects. Adrenaline, however, is a short-term drug, and after a period of time, you are forced to relax. We did and began to talk. Our discussions turned to the mindset of the villagers and the goals of the insurgents. Clearly the insurgents could not operate without some measure of support from the villagers. Whether that support was voluntary or coerced was unclear and it often changed. Coalition supporters one day would become insurgents the next, either because they were bribed into joining the insurgency or because they suffered a real or perceived injury from occupying forces.

Our first destination was the Al-Qa'im elementary school, which was located in a remote area of Diyala Province. In order to reach the school, we had to drive across the Tigris River. It was a first for me, and despite the obvious danger, I was excited. The trip lasted over an hour, which was a long time to be out on the road and made us an easy target for anyone who was interested in making a point. I was unable to sit by the window due to security constraints but sat forward in my seat so that I could see. I watched the landscape and was struck by the tragedy that had become Iraq—a place where there were once so many beautiful architectural sites that could have provided the country with millions of tourist dollars were reduced to nothing more than ancient rubble. We entered a village of single-story houses, huts really, made out of mud bricks and plaster that seemed to crumble in the sunlight. The convoy stopped, and I got out of the vehicle, stretching my legs that had cramped during the long ride. The dust stirred up by the convoy coated my mouth. There was no beauty in this place. The living conditions were primitive. There was no vegetation—only sand and bricks. The school was in disrepair. It was a flat building the color of the desert around it, surrounded by piles of dirt. The village leaders who had come to meet us engaged first in the usual introductory chat but quickly moved to the crux of the matter, which was in itself unusual and led me to believe there was a high level of frustration there. The men were animated in their complaints.

People of the Middle East speak with their hands, similar to the people of the Mediterranean and very unlike Americans. The more emphatic the speech, the wilder the gesticulations. These men were flailing their arms around, infusing their words with anger, almost threatening. From my point of view, the translating was easy. There was no need to use any interpretive phraseology; the leaders were making themselves abundantly clear. They insisted there were not enough classrooms to provide instruction to all of the school-aged children, and in any event, there was no electricity or running water, making the classrooms almost unusable. The leaders accused US Army personnel and representatives from the Iraqi Ministry of Education of doing little to help the school, which of course was not true. At least with regard to the Americans, we were doing a great deal, but our Iraqi partners often undercut the process. As I listened to the words and repeated them in English, I wondered how we would accomplish our mission of winning hearts and minds. Clearly the Iraqis had grown impatient with the progress of reconstruction.

Whether the fault lay with the insurgents or with bureaucratic inertia did not seem to concern them. The facts of their lives required immediate assistance. It was imperative that we impress upon the villagers that notwithstanding the pace of the reconstruction, the coalition had done more to improve their lives than the insurgents had. It was a tough sell.

The struggle for power was apparent in almost every visit I made to the villages. More than once, village leaders complained of bureaucratic roadblocks or corruption. There were constant complaints that the United States was not doing enough. There was not enough electricity, or the water purification plants were not servicing a large enough area. To his credit, my first commander possessed a reserve of calm I have yet to witness in any other human. He listened carefully and never made any promises. His favorite phrase was, "I will look into it," and to my knowledge, he always did.

The assistant chief of staff for civil affairs of the 13th Corps Support Command (COSCOM) and the soldiers under his command represented, to me, the antithesis of the struggle for power in Iraq. Under his command, in 2004, COSCOM sponsored over $4 million worth of infrastructure improvements, including school reconstruction, medical-clinic construction, and water-treatment projects in the villages surrounding LSA Anaconda. Unfortunately, it sometimes seemed that the civil affairs units were working at odds with other parts of the armed forces.

The men and women with whom I worked were dedicated to building bridges, both figuratively and literally. We worked to help build and rebuild schools, water-purification plants, and oil and fuel plants. It was gratifying much of the time, but the level of frustration and the sense of futility grew the longer I stayed.

Later, we met with the teachers of the school and some of the children and gave them some school supplies and promises of future assistance. It is always the children that fueled the anger, the frustration, and the desire to help. The children are the great equalizers. Each side cites their future as the justification for all they do. The problem is that all sides define success differently, and until we can all agree on what is best for the children, it seems we will be forever caught up in this tempest. We did not stay long, and we did little other than observe and make promises that the Iraqis did not believe. The trip to the second school on our itinerary should have been short, but the roads were circuitous and not well marked, so we got lost along the way.

Our security detail was getting jumpy. Many have heard of the disasters that have struck those unlucky enough to make a wrong turn, including the now infamous story of the capture and recovery of private Jessica Lynch.[1] None of us was interested in becoming the next day's headlines. While our driver and navigator were reviewing maps and GPS coordinates, I noticed a group of Iraqis working in the field next to the road. Even in the stress of the moment, I was drawn to the difficulties facing these people. In a country that could afford to build a billion-dollar oil industry and government palaces, these people were eking out a living digging the land with handheld hoes. Much to the surprise of my companions, I decided to approach the farmers and ask for directions. I stepped out of the Humvee, careful to keep my hands at my sides, and walked over slowly. I introduced myself in Arabic, and before asking for help, keeping in mind the cultural necessities of introduction, I asked them about their families and their children. Having obviously shown them respect, they willingly guided us in the right direction, adding caution to be careful because there had been an explosion in the area not too many days before. I thanked them, and we moved on, much to the relief of all of my traveling companions.

We finally arrived at the Muhammed Abdu school, which was essentially uninhabitable. According to the school guards and representatives of the village, classes were being held outside. The villagers complained that the contractor responsible for rebuilding basically took the money and ran; he did little to no work, and there had been no adequate repairs made in months. In addition, we heard complaints that the village did not have enough electricity to maintain satisfactory living conditions.

Once again, we listened, took notes, and made promises. The problems seemed overwhelming; there did not seem to be enough money, time, or sense of loyalty among the citizens to make the transition into a healthy, working society. On our way back to the base, we got lost again, but this time the GPS device was sufficient to guide the way. As we were driving, we passed the Al-Ashraf camp. I was fascinated. The camp had been used by the Iranian Mujahedin al-Khalq. It is a group with a long, sordid past. To some, they are considered allies of the West, and to others, they are the basest kind of killers and charlatans. According to Michael Rubin in his detailed and well-researched article "Monsters of the Left," the Mujahedin al-Khalq, or the MKO, has done an excellent public relations job of presenting themselves as supporters of democracy in general and US policy in Iran in particular. Rubin insists that the MKO is a terrorist organization that sought to replace Khomeini's dictatorship with a dictatorship of its own. According to him, the MKO opposed the Islamic revolution in Iran only after Ayatollah Khomeini purged them from power.[2] Nonetheless, the group supported the Kurds in their uprising against Saddam Hussein, and in August 2003 exposed Iran's covert nuclear enrichment program, thereby earning the gratitude and respect of some members of the United States government.

Iraqi society is filled with monuments to war, heroes, and martyrs. Their stories are rich with imagery and inspire feuds that last millennia. For example, Shi'ite homes are draped with flags of green, black, and red. Green symbolizes Islam; black is the color of mourning for their Imams, all who died during the seventh century; and red signifies revenge against those who killed the Imams. The difference in colors of these flags reflects the historical friction between the Sunnis and Shiites, which took place centuries ago. The Al-Ashraf camp was another symbol of struggle in Iraq, perhaps more recent, but it still inspired deeply held feelings of patriotism or betrayal, depending on which side you belonged.

The second case shows the Iranian group, which has been in opposition to the current Iranian government since the Islamic revolution in Iran and even during the Iran-Iraq war. That's why they were housed at al-Ashraf camp in Iraq.

Not all of my visits were fraught with danger or full of political history, but they were all exceptional with respect to the windows they provided into the soul of the Iraqi people. On my first visit to the village of Albu

Hassan to check the progress of a water purification project, I was struck by the simple sadness of the people. Sadness in Iraq is made of mud and waste and trash and rubble. Sadness is festering puddles and untreated sewage. It infects the children, whose eyes followed the convoy as we drove through the town; and the children in turn infected their mothers, who turned their faces away from us in disgust. As the convoy progressed down the narrow streets, I came to understand the metaphor of sweet-smelling air because of the contrast to it there. Even in my memory, I am nauseated by the stink of that village.

There is a desperate need for clean, fresh, potable water in Iraq. Economic sanctions, war damage, and looting of Iraq's water facilities have led to a crisis in public health. The villagers use untreated water straight from the canals or the Tigris and Euphrates Rivers, leading to epidemics of typhoid and dysentery. Among the primary missions of the United States Agency for International Development (USAID) is to construct and rebuild water supply facilities. Although some of the projects reached their goals and were successful, for many others, the same graft and corruption that plagued the school rebuilding projects plagued the water purification projects, leaving illness and disappointment in their wakes.

As if to emphasize the anger expressed by the villagers, we learned upon our return to the base that shortly after we had left, they discovered an unexploded rocket. It had since been diffused, and we were able to reenter. Two months later, I returned to Albu Hassan. The stink was gone, and along with it the sadness that had permeated the place. We visited the school, and I heard children laughing inside the classroom. The school was clean and filled with supplies. The only request was that, at some time in the future, the facility be expanded. As we left, the children ran fearlessly alongside the Humvees, calling out, playing, and seeking the candy and toys that often accompanied visits from Americans. The local sheikh, who is traditionally the leader of the village, was happy to see us and invited us into his home. Although the security detail hoped we would decline the invitation, according to Iraqi custom, to do so would have been considered an insult. The sheikh's home was located next to the now-functioning water purification plant. Remembering my first visit, my stomach lurched into my throat just thinking about eating while surrounded by the smell of raw sewage. But there was no odor any longer. I was able to enjoy the beauty of the area. The hills and narrow streets reminded me of my childhood. The tree trunks were thick and offered welcome shade from the ever-growing heat of the sun. As we drove to the sheikh's residence, I was transported to the hills and lakes of Shusha, to the stone streets and old mosques. As we entered the sheikh's home, we were greeted by his young daughter. Females are often excused from contact with strange men, but she was still considered a child, although not for long. The sheikh explained that it would soon be time for her to put the headscarf on, indicating she was nearing premarriage age. We were led into a large room that obviously served as a living room. Consistent with Shi'ite custom, the room was decorated with religious writings that included the names of all twelve Shi'ite Imams. The sheikh was cordial but commanding in his presence and concern about his tribesmen. He was obviously pleased with the progress of the past two months but insisted more needed to be done. Our commander, for his part, was consistent in his insistence that Iraqis needed to work within the governmental system they had created and rely less on the United States. The sheikh had obviously intended to invite us to a feast and had elaborate dishes prepared in advance for our enjoyment. Food had been transported from Balad for the occasion. We were served kubba, which is a delicious mixture of minced meat with nuts, raisins, and spices, including, I think, saffron and mint. We were served traditional dishes of chicken, beef, and lamb, as pork is prohibited. The meal ended with baklava and Iraqi tea that was served in small glasses without milk and sweetened with sugar. As we left, the sheikh thanked us for all that had been done to help his village, and my commander promised as much support as possible for future projects.

Successes are hard-fought in Iraq, but the effects of endless war are slowly eroding them. As I read newspapers today, I am afraid the stink will return to Albu Hassan and with it the sadness and anger. Then I wonder if all the work and the sacrifice will have been a terrible waste. I thought I understood the Iraqis in a way that maybe most Americans did not. I thought I understood why they bristled under coalition control. It is hard for an American to understand what it is like to live under the thumb of an invading power. Instead of pride and patriotism, there is an overwhelming sense of loss. There is a sense of powerlessness that your destiny does not belong to you. It is not really a sense of dread, but rather a sense of surrender or resignation. But still, living can only be obtained from life-giving activities: from safety, health, and economic stability. Perhaps when there has been enough death to satisfy the hunger for revenge of the warring, they will stop, and the building will begin.

On March 7, 2005, we were on another mission. We would be visiting three villages: 14 Ramadan, Al-Betera, and Al-Ouabaitar. There were projects we financially supported in all three villages. All of them were almost completed. The purpose of the site visits was to make sure that everything was going well and to talk to the leaders and residents of the villages. Besides, just talking to the Iraqis and listening to their needs and their problems went a long way. I can always see in their eyes that they appreciate it, and I am sure that it would definitely pay off in the long run on this trip. This was about winning the hearts and minds of the Iraqis, which was not at all less important than military and security operations in the country.

In the village of Al-Betera, a little boy came up to me and asked me to give him some money. I looked at him and noticed that he didn't have shoes, his feet were caked in mud and dirt, and his clothing was very old and ripped. I gave him money and I asked where his parents were. He said that his father had died and his mother was sick. I asked him if he had brothers and sisters. He showed me a little girl standing in the distance, looking at us. He said that this was his sister and she was also hungry. I got some candies and cookies from the Humvee and gave them to the kids. The boy then asked me to visit his mother because she was very sick and needed help. He showed me a very remote house in the distance and asked me to come with him. I was about to ask my commanders for permission to go with him, but at that moment, we received an order to leave. The mission was over.

Later, when I tell other people about this incident, I am told that the boy's invitation to the house might have been a trap by the insurgents. The order to leave right then may have prevented me from getting killed or taken hostage. Who knows what the reality of that situation was? I am still not sure. I frequently see those two little kids in my dreams; they look at me and beg me to come with them to their house. I go to their house and enter it. It is very dark inside. Then the boy, with the voice of an adult, tells me not to be afraid and to come.

He goes inside and I follow him. At the end of the room I see a sick woman in a bed. Her eyes are closed, and she is very pale. The boy tells her, "Mom, he came; open your eyes." The woman opens her big eyes and, suddenly, she asks me with a coughing and scary voice, "Why are you here? Why did you come to Iraq?" I look at the boy and the boy is laughing at me, but his sister is crying. Then I look at the woman. Her eyes are closed again. Usually at that moment, I wake up.

After I received my US citizenship in 2006, Senator Jim Inhofe from Oklahoma, who was the ranking member of the Arms Services Committee, invited me to his office and thanked me for my service in Iraq. We took a picture together, and the senator signed it: "Mahir-Great American." The picture is now on the wall of my house and is one of my favorites. I was very impressed with the senator and his dedication and patriotism, and I hope he and others will always consider me a "great American."

9

Homeland

In an era of globalization, internet networking, and instant access to worldwide news media when the merging or partnering of ideological groups is increasingly opposing the United States and/or its policies, the US Army will have to operate in pan-regional and multiregional battle spaces comprised of numerous cultures, both friendly and hostile. The operational environment (OE) of our troops will likely be characterized by persistent and unpredictable conflicts in battle spaces teeming with multiple foreign cultures, exacerbated by the possibility of large-scale combat operations and threats from adversaries such as China and Russia during the next decade.

To meet these operational and cultural challenges, the army's goal, as defined in the Army Culture and Foreign Language Strategy (ACFLS) published on December 1, 2009, is to develop and maintain expeditionary forces that are led by soldiers who are ready to deploy and operate effectively anywhere in the world across the full spectrum of conflict.

In March 2009, prior to the publication of the strategy, I was hired at Fort Sill in Lawton, Oklahoma, as the first US Army Training and Doctrine Command (TRADOC) cultural and foreign language advisor, based on a 2008 directive by then Training and Doctrine Command commander general William Wallace. I was told that there were two main reasons that led to my selection for the job. First, the new culture and foreign-language strategy envisioned a global approach, mostly for the general-purpose force, which perfectly fit my multicultural and multilingual background and expertise. Secondly, I was already at Fort Sill working as a culture and language advisor for a defense contractor. The Fort Sill program was so successful that accreditors suggested it become a model for the rest of the army. Success of the program was also possible to a greater extent thanks to the appreciation of and very effective support of Fort Sill leadership such as the deputy to the commanding general Kirby Brown, Major General Ross Ridge, and many others. As a result, I was awarded the Commander's Award for Civilian Service and the army promoted and moved me to the Combined Arms Center (CAC) at Fort Leavenworth as the senior culture and foreign language advisor with the guidance to replicate the success at Fort Sill TRADOC and army wide.

In 2011, when the CAC began taking over the role of the army's Culture and Foreign Language Program, most of the CAC's centers of excellence started to hire culture and foreign-language advisers. I was the senior among such advisers and was responsible for overall implementation of the army's culture and foreign-language strategy (ACFLS) across TRADOC and the army. Once again, as we had done before at Fort Sill, a unique and effective approach with a specific implementation plan and assessment mechanism was developed at Fort Leavenworth in support the culture and language-strategy implementation, but good ideas were lost amid the subsequent politics and bureaucracy that had created impediments and redundancy. One of the main problems was that the army officially established a related office at Fort Leavenworth, which was comprised of a culture and foreign-language advisor, one military person, and me as the senior culture and foreign-language advisor but did not close the previously functioning office at TRADOC headquarters. This created a lot of difficulties toward completing our mission at Fort Leavenworth during the next several years, effectively impeding the army's intended mission at Fort Leavenworth. Experience at Fort Sill, as one particular military base, was very different, because leadership effectively supported our ideas and efforts and politics was not an impeding or prevailing factor.

In April 2013, my official term as a US Department of Defense (Intergovernmental Personnel Act/IPA) employee expired, and I was about to leave the job and was searching for other opportunities. During the search for a job, I learned that a new position of a program manager for culture and foreign language was advertised at Fort Leavenworth. I kept applying for different jobs and this one was one of them. I needed to quickly find a job so that I could support my family but wanted one that was hopefully in line with my education and professional skills. To my surprise, I was selected, and as I learned later, I was chosen out of many other applicants. I became the manager for the US Army program for assessing language, regional expertise, and culture (LREC), later rebranded by the army leadership as the program for culture, regional expertise, and language (CREL), emphasizing the priority of understanding cultures over foreign-language proficiency, mostly because of the size of the army, the global nature of the general conventional force, and the high cost of foreign-language training.

My responsibilities included coordinating and conducting CREL events in support of the army's ACFLS implementation across TRADOC. I also served as the lead agent for ACFLS at the army's Leader Development Forum, and I was responsible for the coordination and synchronization of policy, doctrine, and resources for CREL requirements. I served as the chair of the Army Learning Coordination Council for culture and joint, interagency, and multinational operations, to synchronize and coordinate learning across TRADOC schools and centers of excellence.

Russia's annexation of Crimea and subsequent violence in Eastern Ukraine had directly affected regional and global geopolitics. The chief of staff of the army (CSA) initiated an army study called the "Russian New Generation Warfare," which required I travel with a small group of US Army professionals to Ukraine in 2016 to follow up with recommendations to army leadership based on our observations. This mission was initiated in response to a changing operational environment as a result of a growing concern over the Russian intentions in the region and challenges for US national security.

The Ukraine I saw was not the same one I had visited right after the Chernobyl nuclear power-plant accident. I was accompanying a Middle Eastern delegation from Moscow to Ukraine as a former Soviet Middle East expert and Arabic interpreter then, when the USSR still officially existed and Ukraine was part of it.

While passing by in the tour bus, the guide showed us the site of the accident in the distance. It was covered by white plastic and obviously continued its deadly spread of nuclear dust, causing cancer across not only Ukraine but also neighboring countries such as Byelorussia, affecting generations to come.

Our trip to Ukraine in 2016 coincided with May 9, Victory Day, which includes celebrations of the defeat of Nazi Germany during the Great Patriotic War of the Soviet Union from 1941 to 1945. We witnessed people still widely celebrating it on the main Khreschatyk Street in central Kiev. We stayed in the Western-style intercontinental hotel but traveled to different sites and meetings. Despite aspirations for independence and anti-Russian patriotic rhetoric, many people still spoke Russian and still had strong cultural ties with Russia. I realized that these strong historical, sociocultural, and linguistic bonds between the two peoples have intertwined so deeply that it would be difficult to break them. This common cultural and linguistic tendency is being actively leveraged by Russia in its ongoing "soft power" activities in Ukraine and other regions of the post-Soviet and post–Warsaw Pact space. We observed many other issues such as of failing economy and prostitution, as well as the first signs of possible lost hearts and minds of the populace by the West, although it was in the early stages of its relationship with Ukraine.

One evening, we went to a restaurant to have dinner. There were a couple of young people at the next table. I was the only one among the group who spoke Russian. After they learned that we were Americans, they said with a smile: "Did you come to Ukraine to store your country's nuclear waste on our land?"

On a different day, per the suggestion of a colleague I will call Colonel X, we went to a disco club in central Kiev. As soon as we entered, a woman named Rita approached me and stayed next to me, constantly showing me attention and affection for the rest of the evening. I tried to keep myself neutral, since I am married and was in front of my teammate. Also, I have a daughter about her age, and that was another reason I tried to keep distance between us. I don't believe her intentions were meant to be sexual. Maybe given the age difference, Rita simply needed comfort from me as a father. But frankly, it did not seem to be the case.

After we left the club, Colonel X told me that Rita's affection was obvious, which was difficult to ignore. Rita probably was in her twenties, much younger than I was, and that was another reason I tried to stay away. I have attributed her behavior to the difficult economic and moral state of Ukrainians and especially young people who were going through periods of hardship, war, and moral crises. Maybe she simply felt morally and mentally comfortable just being around me, because she had told me before I left that I was a very intelligent person. I smiled and replied that she did not know me at all, having met me for the first time. In the following days, Colonel X suggested going back and visiting Rita, but I refused and never went back.

After my return from Ukraine, I led a related major army publication project on the region. The study and related trip to Ukraine were the highlights of my career working for the army.

Similar to the September 11, 2001, terrorist attacks, which prompted interest in my Middle Eastern expertise, related language proficiency, and a subsequent deployment to Iraq, the situation in and around Ukraine, Syria, the Baltics, and so on resulted in a lot of reassessment and discussion of the rapidly changing geopolitical environment and emerging threats.

Once again, I became an active part of those discussions because of my Russian and Eurasian expertise and proficiency in related regional languages, including Russian. Along with senior state department representatives, I was invited as a keynote speaker at the Commander's Conference May 17 and 18, 2016, at Fort Bragg, North Carolina, which was hosted by then Lieutenant General Stephen J. Townsend. The conference provided insight into ISIS, the situation in Syria, and Russian policies in the Middle East and the former USSR. At the request of then Major General James Linder, commanding general of the Special Operations Center of Excellence, I also attended the Russian Engagement in the "Gray Zone" Symposium, which took place in Washington, DC, on October 19 and 20, 2016. Participants included military leadership, US Department of State senior representatives, distinguished scholars, research institutes, practitioners, and other interested parties who were brought together from across the nation to discuss Russia's role in today's gray zone environment. I was one of the main presenters at the first round table discussion, titled "What Is the Importance of Understanding Russian Power Projection and Statecraft and How Does It Shape Russian New Generation Warfare?" I was asked to share my expertise and past experiences related to Eurasia as it applied to the gray zone's operational environment and its implications for regional and global geopolitics. The symposium was well received and attended. Participants emphasized that most importantly, it was a timely event. I was also invited to present at the Fires Symposium on December 14 and 15, 2016, on the subject "Operations-Decisive Action with Regards to Russian Doctrine." These are just examples of the many high-level speaking engagements I was part of, mostly by request.

Since my move to Fort Leavenworth in 2011, in addition to my book *Invitation to Rain: A Story of the Road Taken towards Freedom*, I published two more books: *Life Looking Death in the Eye: The Iraqi War as Experienced by a U.S. Army Contractor* in 2012 and *Cultural Perspectives, Geopolitics & Energy Security of Eurasia: Is the Next Global Conflict Imminent?* in 2017; the second volume, *Great Power Competition: The Changing Landscape of Global Geopolitics*, was published in November 2020. This book will be my fifth one in this country.

At the same time, my efforts as the program manager of the Culture, Regional Expertise, and Language Management Office (CRELMO) and later director of the Cultural and Area Studies Office (CASO) of the US Army Command and General Staff College (CGSC) continue to include a series of seminars or panel discussions on issues of operational and strategic importance to the United States, which the US Army's CASO CGSC, in coordination and jointly with universities, think tanks, interagency and other partners, broadcasts quarterly through video teleconference (VTC) across army schools, Centers of Excellence, Regionally Aligned Forces (RAF), Security Forces Assistance Brigades (SFAB), and other deployed and deploying units, universities, think tanks, and joint, interagency, multinational (JIM) partners and beyond, with an average of 20 to 30 percent of participants following up with feedback, questions, comments, and the impact on their missions. The combined VTC CASO's YouTube and Facebook videos, related publications, and other information are usually accessed after the sessions by thousands at different times.

CASO's Mission and Vision Statement says:

> CGSC Cultural & Area Studies Office (CASO) serves the educational mission within the institution and across the Army. CASO, in conjunction with partner organizations, provides a mechanism to engage all CGSC constituencies concerning the importance of cultural, political, economic and social factors in shaping the operational environment. CASO outreach extends across the Army with

a variety of educational programs, including publishing, guest speakers, direct support to CGSC classes, live panels, video podcasts, international cooperation and research. CASO and its events create a sustainable advantage for Regionally Aligned Forces, Security Forces Assistance Brigades, Army schools and Centers of Excellence by providing training and education tools that enhance Professional Military Education, Pre-Deployment and Functional Training in support of the US National Security and National Defense Strategy objectives in a variety of regional contingencies across the spectrum of conflict including the possibility of Large-Scale Combat Operations. CASO's purpose is to assist in preparing globally responsive and regionally aligned forces that work with a variety of partners including host nation militaries and populations to execute the Army's Prevent, Shape and Win strategic role.[1]

Conclusion

The operational challenges in Afghanistan, Iraq, Syria, and elsewhere are extreme; the strategic implications for all of Eurasia are profound. Fighting forces of the United States must understand the history and use British, Soviet, and other sociocultural lessons learned in Afghanistan, Iraq, Bosnia, and other countries and regions and, at the same time, understand the strategic effects operations may have in the region in order to achieve success. This calls for military leaders and soldiers to acquire a sophisticated set of skills that are different from those of the Cold War era. Leaders and soldiers must understand the context of factors influencing the joint, interagency, and multinational operational environment.

These people must act within the contexts they find themselves, always assessing and adapting their actions based on the interactions and circumstances of the enemy and environment. The military must be able to fluidly transition from one type of operation to another based upon the assessed circumstances while consolidating operational opportunities with the strategic enterprise.[1] At the same time, we need to realistically reassess the possible strategic implications of the wars in Iraq, Afghanistan, and Syria and a new emerging US role in a changing geopolitical landscape.

Based on careful review of the global and regional literature and thorough analysis, one can come to the conclusion that the active military involvement of the United States in Iraq, Afghanistan, Syria, and elsewhere could be the last US wars overseas. The analysis and related information point to the possibility that, by the end of those major conflicts, the United States will no longer be a sole superpower.

The gradual and steady fall of the US dollar, a huge US budget deficit, the colossal and unexpected expenses of the wars, and most importantly lack of clear US strategy and the steady decrease of support at home and popularity abroad—all these among others are clear indicators of a steady trend. The leaders of insurgency and terrorist organizations have indicated that US involvement in the wars in Afghanistan and Iraq was a carefully thought-out plan. In at least two separate statements, Osama Bin Laden acknowledged the existence of such a plan, to make the US economy "bleed" like they made the former Soviet Union "bleed" before its demise.[2]

It is becoming increasingly clear that it is not possible to completely defeat insurgency and terrorism. Their cells can be destroyed and financial support can be cut off. However, other similar kinds of organizations will emerge in their place unless the geopolitical reasons causing insurgency and terrorism are resolved. History repeats itself over and over. The latest developments around Afghanistan, when an "'agreement in principle' [was] reached with [the] Taliban to withdraw 5,000 U.S. troops within five months," indicates that this premise and related analysis might be accurate.[3]

The tension in the Middle East, including in Syria, continues to affect regional and global security. The unresolved Israeli–Palestinian conflict continues to be in the center of many regional conflicts, directly or indirectly. To defuse tension, there should be a more balanced policy toward Israel and its Arab neighbors. As a part of the solution of the Israeli–Palestinian conflict, there should be the creation of two states: Israel and Palestine.

The futures of Iraq and Afghanistan should be decided by the people of these countries, with the help of the international community and international organizations, such as the United Nations. Otherwise, the involvement of other countries unilaterally will always be perceived as interference, and it will further cause alienation, thus creating a basis for insurgency and terrorism. Terms such as *insurgency*, *terrorism*, and so on need to be clearly defined and leveraged in the right narrative context. Otherwise, it will only create confusion and a basis for the emergence of new violent groups and organizations with their own political agendas. It is very important to define the differences among *insurgency*, *terrorism*, and other terms.

The recent Azerbaijani-Armenian full-scale war and the terms of the subsequent peace deal have clearly highlighted a rapidly changing geopolitical landscape in the Caucasus, which would inevitably have long-lasting implications for the entire post-Soviet and post–Warsaw Pact space and the role of international organizations.

In addition to Russia, as a traditional player in its centuries' old backyard, Turkey has emerged as another leading power with a steadily expanding role in regional and global geopolitics.

Given all these factors, the next few decades will most likely see the United States lose its sole grip on world affairs, and new superpowers will emerge. One of the likely candidates is China, which has successfully managed to modify its political and economic systems to the requirements of the present time. In the new era, the most effective factors of influence are going to be economic "soft power," "sharp power," and other similar avenues of influence rather than traditional military means.

Another example could be Russia, which has effectively used a combination of economic expansionist policy, "soft power," and military capabilities toward its neighbors, the former Soviet Republics, the Middle East, the Western Hemisphere, and other regions of the world for the past several years. The approaches and actions of major global countries, such as China and Russia, and regional players, such as Iran, North Korea, Saudi Arabia, and Turkey, would not be the same and would be influenced by their respective strategic cultures and mindsets, shaped over centuries and generations. The world is gradually approaching a very dangerous point of conflicting interests and spheres of interests with similar trends, which have led to two world wars and smaller conflicts before. The important distinction of our present reality is that the multiple global and regional players possess nuclear weapons, and the nuclear containment of the Cold War era between the two superpowers is not a factor anymore.

More than ever, the right policies and related decisions will depend on appreciation and understanding of the cultures, history, and mentality of other countries and regions.

Epilogue

I am home now after many adventures and dangers. I have realized my dream, and my wife, my daughter, and I are citizens of the United States of America. I visited Azerbaijan shortly after my time in Iraq. My mother was quite old, and her health was impaired. It was important that I see her, and I am glad I did. Three years later, my mother died. My mother and I had a very special relationship. I was the youngest and so held a special place in her heart that my brother and sister recognized and encouraged. When it was clear her time was close, my brother called me and told me to come soon. I made plans to leave the following week.

As my mother's condition worsened, my siblings were able to calm her just by telling her I was on my way. I am comforted by that knowledge and know that my mother felt my presence even though I did not make it to her bedside before she died.

When I eventually arrived to assist with my mother's burial, all three members of the family—my brother, his wife, and their daughter—witnessed an interesting phenomenon and told me about it.

My mother was already in a coma when my brother, with his wife and daughter at her bedside, told her that I was coming. According to all three of them, at that particular moment, my mother opened her eyes and then finally passed away. We all considered that a miracle, which also could be attributed to our strong mutual affection with my mother over all these years.

A lot of changes are taking place in Azerbaijan since my last visit in the summer of 2018. There are signs that one of the oldest territorial conflicts over the Nagorno-Karabakh region might finally be resolved, people can return to their lands, and I can finally visit my grandfather's wonderful, majestic house, which presumably lies in ruins. Hopefully, the situation in Iraq will also be settled in the future and the people of Iraq can live in peace and prosperity.

They are as different as they are the same. I know I have in some small part helped the world come to terms with itself, but in the end, with one very great exception, there is precious little to celebrate. My daughter is an American; she will never know the yoke of communism. She will always be free to pursue her dreams and determine her own fate. If that is the measure of the success in my life, I am satisfied with it.

Notes

Chapter 1. Soldier of the Empire

1. See Igor Vladimirovich Obraztsov, "The Reasons for Dedovshchina and Ways to Prevent It: A Retrospective Analysis," in *Dedovshchina in the Post-Soviet Military: Hazing of Russian Army Conscripts in a Comparative Perspective*, ed. Françoise Daucé and Elisabeth Sieca-Kozlowski (Stuttgart: Ibidem-Verlag, 2006), 105–120.

2. See Richard Galpin, "Russia's Massive Leaning Statue," BBC News, Moscow, accessed September 6, 2019, http://news.bbc.co.uk/2/hi/europe/8040471.stm. It commemorates the Battle of Stalingrad (August 1942 to February 1943), when the Soviet army managed to defeat the German forces, which is widely seen as a turning point in World War II.

3. See Travellerspoint, "Travel Guide Europe/Russia/Southern Russia/Volgograd," Travellerspoint, accessed August 12, 2019, https://www.travellerspoint.com/guide/Volgograd/.

4. See Amie Taylor, "Romance Tours to Russia," *USA Today*, accessed August 12, 2019, https://traveltips.usatoday.com/romance-tours-russia-25425.html.

5. See Orla Guerin, "Armenia, Azerbaijan and Russia sign Nagorno-Karabakh Peace Deal," BBC News, November 10, 2020, https://www.bbc.com/news/world-europe-54882564.

6. From the Azeri language, "the Isa spring," which is the spring named after Isa. See Izzetkhanim Jabarli, "Karabakh in the Everyday Lives of Azerbaijanis," Jam News by Izzetkhanim Jabarli, December 3, 2018, https://jam-news.net/karabakh-in-the-everyday-lives-of-azerbaijanis/.

7. One of the oldest neighborhoods is also known as *ashaghi meydan* or the lower squire in Azeri. It is located in the lower part of the city of Shusha or, as it is often also called, Shusha castle or fortress. The reason it is called torpag meydani, as believed by the people of Shusha, is because it is covered by dirt, compared to the most of the streets of the city, which are covered with stones.

Chapter 2. The Search for Identity

1. See A. Marshall, *Phased Withdrawal, Conflict Resolution and State Reconstruction* (Watchfield: Defence Academy of the UK, 2006), http://www.da.mod.uk/colleges/arag/document-listings/ca/06(29)AM.pdf/view.

Interlude: Demise of the Empire

1. President of the United States, *US National Security Strategy* (Washington, DC: The White House, May 19, 2010), https://www.hsdl.org/?view&did=24251.

2. Secretary of State, the Director of National Intelligence, the Attorney General, the Administrator of the Drug Enforcement Administration, the Administrator of the United States Agency for International Development, and the Secretary of Agriculture, *Report on Progress toward Security and Stability in Afghanistan* (Washington, DC: SS, DNI, AG, ADEA, AUSAID, and SA, November 2010), https://archive.defense.gov/pubs/November_1230_Report_FINAL.pdf.

3. The Department of Defense Report to Congress, *Report on Progress toward Security and Stability in Afghanistan*, November 2010, Report to Congress in accordance with section 1230 of the National Defense Authorization Act for Fiscal Year 2008, Pub. Law 110–181, as amended, https://archive.defense.gov/pubs/November_1230_Report_FINAL.pdf.

4. Commonly used phrase that means to win support and empathy of the indigenous population during military operations.

5. For more information about locals and Mujahedeen, see Andrea Wheatroft, *Infidels: A History of the Conflict between Christendom and Islam* (New York: Random House, 2005); Bernard Lewis, *The Political Language of Islam* (Chicago: University of Chicago Press, 1991).

6. Published July 2009 by the self-proclaimed Islamic Emirate of Afghanistan, "Bylaws for the Mujahedeen," outlines a Taliban code of conduct.

7. Translation by Farooq Babrakzai of the self-proclaimed Islamic Emirate of Afghanistan, "Bylaws for the Mujahedeen," section on asylum, 2009.

8. Translation by Babrakzai, "Bylaws for the Mujahedeen," section on prisoners, 2009.

9. Translation by Babrakzai, "Bylaws for the Mujahedeen," section on civilian casualties, 2009.

10. Translation by Babrakzai, "Bylaws for the Mujahedeen," section on suicide attacks.

11. See Malawi Hafiz Allah Haqqani, *Taliban: From the Dream of Mullah to Emirate Almoamineen (State of Believers)*, 1st ed. (Islamabad: Political Studies Institute, 1997).

12. This is an English translation of some quotes from the speeches of Mullah Omar in 2009. These quotes are also part of the bylaws, translated by Farooq Babrakzai. The audio link with English subtitles is available at https://www.bing.com/videos/search?q=speeches+of+mullah+omar+in+2009&docid=607986641623582012&mid=d40601ab4f7fa081bae5d40601ab4f7fa081bae5&view=detail&form=vire. See also Mark Schone, "Taliban Leader's Holiday Message: No Peace Talks, 'Focus on the Invaders,'" ABC News, November 25, 2009, https://abcnews.go.com/Blotter/taliban-releases-holiday-message/story?id=9176747/.

13. Islamic Emirate of Afghanistan, "Bylaws for the Mujahedeen," trans. Farooq

Babrakzai, Laghman, 2009. Published by the self-proclaimed Islamic Emirate of Afghanistan, the bylaws outlines a Taliban code of conduct. Please also see "Taliban Issues Code of Conduct: Document for Fighters Outlines Treatment of Hostages and Use of Suicide Bombers," Al Jazeera, July 28, 2009, https://www.aljazeera.com/news/2009/7/28/taliban-issues-code-of-conduct.

14. In traditionally Muslim countries, Islam is considered an integral part of society, the "way of life." Across history, this aspect could play different roles in political agendas within society and in international relations. The role of the Islamic factor in international relations has attracted the attention of American and Western experts in relationship to contemporary Islam. Islam has become a significant political phenomenon, not only in internal political and social lives of traditionally Islamic countries, beginning in the 1950s and 1970s after they gained their independence, but in current international relations as well. The "Islamic Revivalism" of the 1970s and 1980s mainly consisted of three components, which were the Islamic revolution in Iran, events in and around Afghanistan, and the activation of the Muslim organizations and movements around the world. This period also witnessed the first signs of unification of some anti-Western regimes in the Middle East. As a result, these events have significantly changed the character of international relationships between the traditionally Muslim world and the West.

15. The Baʿath Party, Baʿath, Baʿth in full Arab, the Socialist Baʿath Party, Arab Socialist Renaissance Party, Arabic Ḥizb al-Baʿath al-ʿArabī al-Ishtirākī, or Pan-Arabist political party advocates the formation of a single Arab socialist nation and is not based on Islamism. It is based on an Arab nationalistic agenda.

16. "Profile: Gulbuddin Hekmatyar," BBC News, March 23, 2010, http://news.bbc.co.uk/2/hi/middle_east/2701547.stm.

17. Ahmed Rashid, *Taliban: Militant Islam, Oil and Fundamentalism in Central Asia* (New Haven, CT: Yale University Press, 2001).

18. Tariq Mahmood, "Durand Line: South Asia's New Trouble Spot" (diss., Army BSc [Honors] War Studies, Balochistan University, Pakistan, 1996).

19. See Robert M. Cassidy, *War, Will, and Warlords* (Quantico, VA: Marine Corps University Press, 2012), 10. Pashtunwali can be interpreted as "the way of the Pashtuns" or "a kind of moral code." It is widely practiced among Pashtun tribes.

20. Aljazeera.net (in Arabic) report published in October 2004 based its information on Malawi Hafiz Allah Haqqani, *Taliban: From the Dream of Mullah to Emirate Almoamineen (State of Believers)*, 1st ed. (Islamabad: Political Studies Institute, 1997).

21. Former ambassador John J. Maresca, "Testimony to the House Subcommittee on Asia and the Pacific, February 12, 1998," *Ratville Times*, accessed December 13, 2020, https://ratical.org/ratville/CAH/linkscopy/Maresca2USG.html.

22. "Drugs Finance Taliban War Machine, Says UN Drug Tsar," United Nations Office of Drugs and Crime Control, November 27, 2008, https://www.unodc.org/unodc/en/press/releases/2008-11-27.html.

Chapter 4. A Socialist Democracy

1. The Freedom Support Act of 1992 is an act passed by the United States Congress. The FSA was signed into law on October 24, 1992, by president George H. W. Bush. See Freedom for Russia and Emerging Eurasian Democracies and Open Markets Support Act of 1992, H.R. 4547, 102nd Cong. (March 24, 1992), https://www.congress.gov/bill/102nd-congress/house-bill/4547. See also Ben Barber, "New Senate Panel Chief Aims to Slash Foreign Aid," *Washington Times*, December 13, 1994; and Mahir Ibrahimov and Erjan Kurbanov, "Policy Brief: Getting It Wrong in the Caucausus," *Middle East Quarterly* (December 1994): 65–70.

2. "Senate Foreign Relations Committee Report on the Passage by the Committee of Freedom Support Act," October 1992.

3. See Ambassador John J. Maresca, "U.S. Ban on Aid to Azerbaijan (Section 907): How It Started in 1992 and Why It Should Be Lifted," *Azerbaijan International* 6, no. 4 (Winter 1998): 54–55.

4. Middle East Studies Association, "Mission Statement," Middle East Studies Association of North America, Inc., accessed October 24, 2020, https://mesana.org/.

Chapter 6. The Real Weapon of Mass Destruction

1. Peter Bouckaert and Fred Abrahams, "Violent Response: The U.S. Army in Al Falluja," Human Rights Watch, June 2003, https://www.hrw.org/reports/2003/iraqfalluja/.

2. "The Iraq War: Fallujah Before and After," World Press, accessed on May 8, 2020, https://articlesfactsstats.wordpress.com/the-iraq-war-fallujah-before-and-after/.

3. Esther Pan, "Iraq: Justifying the War," Council on Foreign Relations, February 2, 2005, https://www.cfr.org/backgrounder/iraq-justifying-war.

4. Austin J. Luckenbach, "Iraq and Afghanistan: Similar, Yet Different," *Small Wars Journal*, August 30, 2015, https://smallwarsjournal.com/jrnl/art/iraq-and-afghanistan-similar-yet-different.

5. Ahmed S. Hashim, *Insurgency and Counter-Insurgency in Iraq* (Ithaca, NY: Cornell University Press and London: C. Hurst, 2006).

6. Formerly Kellogg, Brown & Root, KBR, Inc., is an American engineering, procurement, and construction company, formerly a subsidiary of Halliburton.

7. Peter W. Singer, *Corporate Warriors: The Rise of the Privatized Military Industry* (Ithaca, NY: Cornell University Press, 2003).

Chapter 7. Clash of Cultures and Casualties of War

1. The lessons of foreign wars are usually collateral damage, which means unintentional civilian casualties among the civilian population during military operations. It

significantly contributes to the loss of the hearts and minds of the populace. It could ultimately lead to the loss of the war while still winning the battle at some point. We saw it with former British experiences in British India (now Pakistan), the Soviet invasion of Afghanistan, and other examples. Also, if a foreign country invades another foreign country, even when done with good intentions, it is very easy for different groups in that country, in the region and so on to justify their political agendas, utilizing religious, nationalistic, or other ideologies to fuel insurgency.

Chapter 8. Rising with Hope from Ashes

1. Jessica Dawn Lynch (born April 26, 1983) is a former United States Army soldier who served in the 2003 invasion of Iraq by US and allied forces. On March 23, 2003, Private First Class Lynch was serving as a unit supply specialist with the 507th Maintenance Company when her convoy was ambushed by Iraqi forces during the Battle of Nasiriyah. Lynch was seriously injured. Her subsequent recovery by US Special Operations Forces on April 1, 2003, received considerable media coverage.

2. Michael Rubin, "Monsters of the Left," *Front Page Magazine*, American Enterprise Institute, January 13, 2006.

Chapter 9. Homeland

1. US Army Combined Arms Center, "Cultural and Area Studies Office (CASO) –Previously CRELMO: Mission and Vision Statement," US Army, accessed March 21, 2019, https://usacac.army.mil/organizations/cace/lrec/.

Conclusion

1. Mahir Ibrahimov, "Socio-cultural Lessons from Eurasia and Afghanistan," *Military Intelligence Professional Bulletin* (MIPB), February 9, 2011. Also see Mahir Ibrahimov, "Operational Culture in the U.S. Army: The Fires Center of Excellence Culture and Foreign Language Strategy Sets the Standard for the rest of TRADOC, Army," Fires, January–February 2011, 23.

2. Mahir Ibrahimov, *Life Looking Death in the Eye: The Iraqi War as Experienced by a U.S. Army Contactor* (New York: Global Scholarly Publications, 2012). See also Osama Bin Laden, "Nass Bayan al-Jabhah al-Islamiyah al-Alamiyah li-Jihad al-Yahud wa-al-Salibiyin" (World Islamic front for jihad against Jews and crusaders), *al-Quds al-Arabi*, February 23, 1998. This is the second Fatwa published in the Arabic newspaper.

3. Deirdre Shesgreen, Tom Vanden Brook, John Fritze, and Nicholas Wu, "'Agreement in Principle' Reached with Taliban to withdraw 5,000 US Troops within Five Months," *USA Today*, September 3, 2019, https://www.usatoday.com/story/news/world/2019/09/02/agreement-principle-reached-taliban-end-afghanistan-war-withdraw-us-troops/2141480001/.

Additional Sources

Although not directly cited, the following publications were influential in the development of the chapters of the book:

"Azerbaycan 24 sene sonra Ermenistan'dan geri aldı" (Azerbaijan returned [lands] from Armenia 24 years later). Milliyet.com, April 25, 2016. https://www.tgrthaber.com.tr/editorun-sectikleri/azerbaycan-24-sene-sonra-ermenistandan-geri-aldi-120720.

Baumann, Robert F. "A Central Asian Perspective on Russian Soft Power: The View from Tashkent." *Military Review*, July–August 2018. https://www.armyupress.army.mil/Journals/Military-Review/English-Edition-Archives/July-August-2018/Baumann-Asian/.

Borshchevskaya, Anna, and Catherine Cleveland. "Russia's Arabic Propaganda: What It Is, Why It Matters." Washington Institute, December 2018. https://www.washingtoninstitute.org/policy-analysis/view/russias-arabic-propaganda-what-it-is-why-it-matters.

Dugin, Alexander. *Eurasian Mission: An Introduction to Neo-Eurasianism*. Budapest: Arktos Media, 2014.

——. *The Fourth Political Theory*. Budapest: Arktos Media, 2012.

Foundation "Russia World." "Home." Russian World Portal. Accessed October 17, 2020. http://www.russkiymir.ru/russkiymir/en/.

Gerasimov, Valery V. *Tsenosti Nauki V Predvidenii. Novie Vizovi Trebuyut Pereosmislit Formi I Sposobi Vedenia Boyevikh Deistviy* (The value of science is in the prediction: New challenges demand rethinking the forms and methods of carrying out combat operations). Voyenno-Promyshlennyy Kurier online, February 27, 2013, http://vpk-news.ru/articles/14632.

Ibrahimov, Mahir J. "Cross-Cultural Negotiations/Skill Building in an Operational Environment." *Military Intelligence Professional Bulletin* (MIPB), April/June 2011. http://usacac.army.mil/sites/default/files/documents/cace/LREC/2011_CrossCulturalNegotiations.pdf.

——. *Invitation to Rain: A Story of the Road Taken towards Freedom*. New York: Global Scholarly Publications, 2008.

——. "Socio-cultural Lessons from Eurasia and Afghanistan." *Military Intelligence Professional Bulletin* (MIPB), January/March 2011. http://usacac.army.mil/sites/default/files/documents/cace/LREC/2011_Socio-CulturalLessons.pdf.

——, Otto Gustav, and Gentile Lee. *Cultural Perspectives, Geopolitics and Energy Secu-*

rity of Eurasia: Is the Next Global Conflict Imminent? US Army Command and General Staff College Press, US Army Combined Arms Center, Fort Leavenworth, Kansas, March 2017.

Meador, Mitch. "Army Built on Fear Remembered by Former Soldier." *Lawton Constitution*, July 28, 2008.

Mehtiyev, Ramiz. "Azerbaijan Halqi Oz Torpaglarinin Ishgal Altinda Galmasi Ila Hech Vaxt Barishmayacag" (Azerbaijan will never agree its lands to remain under occupation). Halq Gezeti in Azerbaijani, April 6, 2016.

"Nord Stream 2 Partners withdraw Amid Poland Pressure." *Financial Times*, August 12, 2016.

Putin, Vladimir V. *Ukaz Prezidenta Rossiyskoy Federatsii o Strategii Natsionalnoy Bezopasnosti Rossiyskoy Federatsii* (The decree of the president of the Russian federation on the national security strategy of the Russian Federation). Moscow, Russia, December 31, 2015. [Signed] Russian Federation President V. Putin Moscow, the Kremlin, No. 683, approved by Russian Federation Presidential Edict 683. http://www.ieee.es/Galerias/fichero/OtrasPublicaciones/Internacional/2016/Russian-National-Security-Strategy-31Dec2015.pdf.

———. *Voyennaya Doctrina Rossiyskoy Federatsii* (The military doctrine of the Russian Federation). December 26, 2014. Approved by the President of the Russian Federation on December 25, 2014, No. Pr.-2976. https://rusemb.org.uk/press/2029.

Theohary, Catherine A. *Information Warfare: Issues for Congress (R45142)*. Congressional Research Service (CRS), ver. 5, updated, March 5, 2018.

World Bank. "GDP Growth (Annual %)." Data Bank, World Development Indicators, accessed September 12, 2016. http://databank.worldbank.org/data/reports.aspx?Code=ny.gdp.mktp.kd.zg&id=af3ce82b&report_name=Popular_indicators&populartype=series&ispopular=y#.